Tadich GRILL

The Story of San Francisco's
Oldest Restaurant, with Recipes

JOHN BRISCOE

Foreword by MICHAEL BUICH

TEN SPEED PRESS
Berkeley / Toronto

⤳ For Carol ⤶

A Kirsty Melville Book

Ten Speed Press
PO Box 7123
Berkeley, California 94707
www.tenspeed.com

Distributed in Australia by Simon and Schuster Australia, in Canada by Ten Speed Press
Canada, in New Zealand by Southern Publishers Group, in South Africa by Real Books,
in Southeast Asia by Berkeley Books, and in the United Kingdom and Europe by Airlift
Book Company.

Cover and text design by Nancy Austin

Library of Congress Cataloging-in-Publication Data
Briscoe, John.
Tadich Grill : the story of San Francisco's oldest restaurant, with recipes / John Briscoe.
 p. cm.
Includes bibliographical references and index.
ISBN 1-58008-425-7
1. Tadich Grill—History. 2. Cookery, American. I. Title.
TX945.5.T33 B75 2002
647.95794'61—dc21   2002003985

First printing, 2002
Printed in Singapore

1 2 3 4 5 6 7 8 9 10 — 06 05 04 03 02

CONTENTS

ACKNOWLEDGMENTS

To the Buich family, the owners of Tadich Grill since 1928, I owe the main acknowledgment. We were friends before this project, and are closer friends now. Steve Buich opened his archive of pictures and memorabilia and researched crannies and arcane corners of the restaurant's history, with the help of his tireless assistant Donna Umeki. Steve and his son Mike, the restaurant's current owners, and Steve's brother Bob also provided anecdotes, information, and introductions to longtime customers.

Doris Muscatine's writings were much help in getting started, especially *A Cook's Tour of San Francisco* and *Old San Francisco*. But the gratitude I owe her is not just for her books. When I was (I thought) well underway with the project, I met Doris and her husband, Charles. We became friends, and Doris was kind enough to read and politely critique several unprintable early iterations.

Carole Vernier, another friend and Herb Caen's longtime assistant, also bestowed patient, civil, and valuable criticism of those early versions of the manuscript.

Bob Hass cajoled me to do this book in the first place, recommending the inclusion of San Francisco's history alongside the Tadich's.

Alev Croutier, author, publisher, and mentor, has been another friend and advisor in this project. Terry Paetzold, chef, teacher, and friend too, has been a marvelous recipe tester (what trying evenings *having* to taste the dishes). Kimberley Cameron, Kirsty Melville, Holly Taines White, and Nancy Austin, agent, publisher, editor, and designer, respectively, have been patient and wise, and patient, and patient.

Thanks too are due Charles Faulhaber and Peter Hanff of the Bancroft Library; Richard Rodriguez, Antonio Rossman, and Mary Risley of Tante Marie's Cooking School in San Francisco; and Tadich head chefs Dave Sokitch, John Canepa, and Fritz Braker. Fritz, the Tadich's current head chef, spent hours with me describing cooking techniques and kitchen-maintenance secrets and, of course, divulging recipes.

When he died in 1999, Louis Claiborne was eulogized as the greatest Supreme Court lawyer of the previous fifty years. He had been my adversary in three cases, my law partner for the last fifteen years of his life, and my children's de facto grandfather. He read and critiqued chapters, and directed me unerringly to the writings of Dumas, Escoffier, his cousin Craig Claiborne, and his friend Ella Brennan.

To others who insidiously implanted in me an affinity for the gastronomic history of San Francisco, I owe a more amorphous acknowledgment. They include my late colleague Edward S. Washburn, my former partner Tom Kemp, Bob and Barbara Cathcart, and the late Joseph L. Alioto. They also include my long-deceased father, John L. Briscoe, who could not take me to Tadich's, Jack's, Sam's, Antoine's, or Brennan's without regaling me with the restaurant's history. I suppose I am carrying out some subtle mandate he left when he died in 1965.

■ 240 California Street, home of Tadich Grill from 1967 to the present.

FOREWORD

Many gastronomes seem to agree with the late Herb Caen's statement, "San Francisco without Tadich Grill would not be San Francisco." Although flattering, the fact is, San Francisco would still be San Francisco without Tadich Grill. San Francisco is, after all, a city that was born some 150 years ago and has undergone so much dramatic change that it certainly would not lose stride with or without one particular business or another. However, just as one can only scratch the surface of a description of our planet without understanding some basics of the solar system in which it exists, one cannot possibly write a history of one of San Francisco's oldest four businesses without including significant information on "The City" itself. (Boudin Bakery was also founded in 1849; Wells Fargo followed in 1852; Levi Strauss in 1853.)

John Briscoe, prominent San Francisco attorney, father, food enthusiast, history buff, and writer, took on a tremendous task six years ago. Had he known then the hours ahead of him on this voyage, he may likely have aborted the mission. But John, exemplifying the true tenacity, determination, and willpower of the city he was born in (San Francisco, of course), and also the same characteristics of those who have owned and operated the business that is the subject of his writings herein, indeed managed to succeed, pressing forward again and again. I wish to thank John for his relentless efforts, as he has, through this book, given a wonderful gift to the city of San Francisco and its many residents and visitors. He has delivered to us all a recount of the history not just of a restaurant, but of one of the world's most vibrant cities, through the kaleidoscope of The Original Cold Day Restaurant.

The tale is a conglomeration of diverse facts, skillfully woven together, offering the reader insights into the history of the city and the evolution of the culinary arts of the West, intertwined with entertaining stories and previously unrecorded details, archival photographs, and classic Tadich recipes.

A great deal of the research that substantiates this story was performed by my father, Steve Buich, and his assistant Donna Umeki, an equally amazing person. Donna, then the restaurant's bookkeeper, worked for my father from 1978 to 1992. During this time, as if there was not already enough to do, the two of them began research on the chronology of the restaurant's ownership and locations. All data up until that time was either from Steve's recollection of stories told by his late father, Louie, and his mother, Mary (Baba to us grandchildren); from senior employees and the many generations of Tadich Grill regulars; or from newspaper clippings that managed to be preserved over the years. Steve and Donna's efforts intensified in 1994 when Steve retired from the business. Being the precise, energetic, type A person that he is, Steve was driven to uncover every detail. He and Donna spent the better part of 1994 through 2000 searching, cross-referencing, discovering, and fitting together each and every piece of a century-plus-old jigsaw puzzle. A series of handmade, embossed leather scrapbooks, twenty by thirty inches in dimension, now house the minutiae they collected, a museum-quality presentation of the history of Tadich Grill. Someday, no doubt, these albums will in fact find their way to a local museum.

Although there are many former owners and employees who should be recognized for their contributions toward the international reputation of Tadich Grill, Steve Buich is without a doubt the single person most responsible for the restaurant's current success. Steve became an owner and the CEO of Tadich's in 1961. Shortly thereafter, in 1965, his father, Louie, died and in 1967 Steve was responsible for moving the restaurant due to the redevelopment of the area. At age thirty-four, he was the driving force behind establishing the restaurant in its present location at 240 California Street. As one examines the business today as closely as I have, the influence of his presence is evident in countless ways; from its method of operation to the decor, there is not one area where he has not left his mark. Steve has been a great mentor and friend, not only to me, but to many of those who have worked with him.

As I touched upon earlier, the employees of Tadich Grill, past and present, are the true champions of this establishment. As any reader with even a summer of restaurant experience will agree, it is a tough business.

When I made my career move from technology in 1989, my father asked me if I was sure I wanted to do this. To which I replied that I was, absolutely. His next comment was, "Okay, but remember there are many easier ways to make a living!" Well again, he was right. But then I wouldn't have had the enjoyment of working with so many dedicated employees, serving so many loyal customers, and carrying on one of the city's treasures for the generations to come.

—Michael Buich

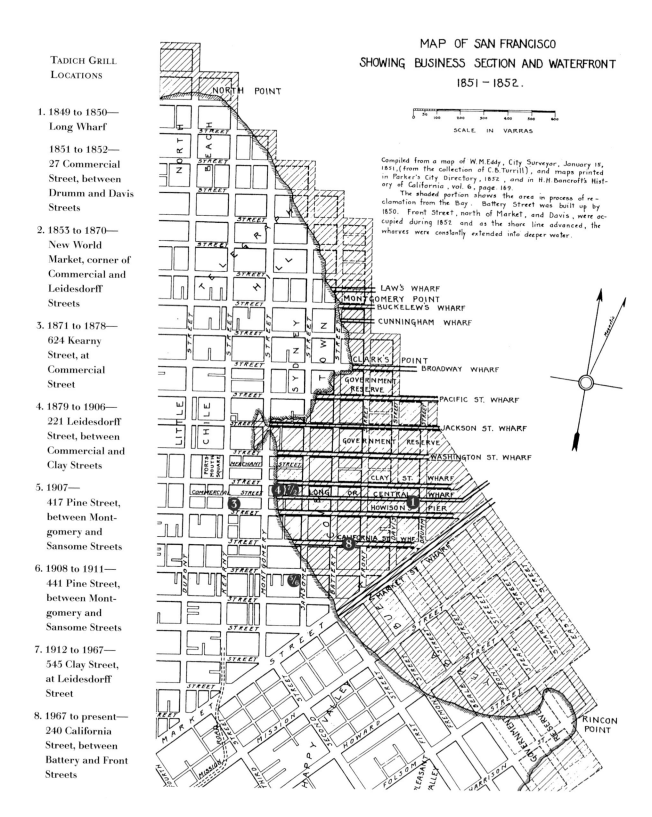

MAP OF SAN FRANCISCO
SHOWING BUSINESS SECTION AND WATERFRONT
1851 – 1852.

SCALE IN VARRAS

Compiled from a map of W.M.Eddy, City Surveyor, January 15,
1851, (from the collection of C.B.Turrill), and maps printed
in Parker's City Directory, 1852, and in H.H.Bancroft's History of California, vol. 6, page 169.
    The shaded portion shows the area in process of re-
clamation from the Bay. Battery Street was built up by
1850. Front Street, north of Market, and Davis, were occupied during 1852 and as the shore line advanced, the
wharves were constantly extended into deeper water.

PREFACE

Tadich Grill, San Francisco's oldest restaurant, has mirrored its city's history, from its founding in 1849, the year of San Francisco's real birth during the gold rush, to its survival of two catastrophic earthquakes. In a way, it has also projected its city's future. It has fed its future mayors when they were young and again years later when they were cutting, over sand dabs, the deals that would decide the city's ever-flamboyant future.

Locals know the restaurant well, but relatively few tourists do, it seems. Those that try it often find themselves put off by its policy of no reservations and by the seemingly interminable wait for a table. But for folks with the savvy to arrive early, the patience to wait for a table, or, better, the wit to take a solitary stool at the counter (there are no tables for one), the reward is the best seafood on the West Coast—and excellent meats and pastas too—unsullied with nouvelle cuisine pretensions. For the out-of-towner with a perch on a counter stool, a further reward is a chat with the San Franciscans seated on the left and right. One may be the city's state senator, or its symphony conductor, the American poet laureate, or the janitor from the building next door. They all eat there. And they couldn't get a table either.

My first memory of Tadich Grill is from August of 1953. San Francisco was an incessant party, nearly on the order, I suppose, of the celebrations following V-J Day in 1945. The Korean War had ended. My uncle Bob, a lieutenant in the army's paratrooper corps, had just fought his second war. When he returned from duty in the Far East, we met him dockside at Fort Mason in San Francisco. I was five, school had not yet begun, and I was taken everywhere Uncle Bob and the other adults went, for what seemed like weeks.

I remember the North Beach places then. North Beach was where we lived, with Mrs. Giacomazzi, who lived another thirty years to the age of 107 and who knew every living person in North Beach. But I also remember Tadich Grill.

I had probably been to the Tadich before, but my earliest recollection is of that August. In Tadich Grill, which in 1953 was at 545 Clay Street, there was a din unlike the din today. There weren't many children there—none that I can remember, at any rate. But adults were crowded shoulder to shoulder, giddy. I remember being handed glasses of Coca-Cola and dishes of ice cream by soldiers and sailors, being hoisted on shoulders, and hugged and talked to and shown pictures by servicemen, all while we waited for a table, I suppose. I knew then that San Francisco, North Beach, and this Tadich Grill were the greatest places on earth. Only many years later, when my own son was serving with the army's First Armored Division, in harm's way, did I get it. That day in the Tadich, I had been every soldier's son who had not been seen in a year, or two, or ever.

It was hard then not to develop a fondness for Tadich Grill.

Later, during what seemed like many years but were really very few, putting on a blue blazer meant lunch at Tadich's (or, occasionally, Jack's or Sam's) with my dad. And stories about the places. The one childhood vacation I remember was by train through the South to New Orleans, where I was my father's dinner companion at Brennan's, Broussard's, and Antoine's. Those dinners, in 1956, led to more stories about restaurants. The blue-blazer bit halted a few years later when my father died. But his stories about New Orleans and San Francisco restaurants, especially about Tadich Grill, stuck.

In the mid-1960s, as a college student, I became enthralled with San Francisco's history, and I resumed eating at the Tadich as often as I could afford to. I once interviewed Herb Caen, the great *San Francisco Chronicle* columnist, for a term paper on post-1906 San Francisco. (The paper virtually wrote itself from the tape-recorded interview.) Caen spoke with undisguised affection for the Tadich, for its food and for its remarkable longevity. A few years later, when I began working for a living in downtown San Francisco, I made it a point to eat at the Tadich more often. There were frequently celebrities there, as well as others who were not celebrities but were well known by the owners and staff, and hundreds of plain people like me. Somehow, I probably thought, just eating there, in clamorous anonymity, made me more a San Franciscan.

The Tadich is a busy place. It seats a hundred people at a time and serves eight hundred meals a day. That leaves little time for idle chitchat with the owners and staff. Still, in the 1970s and 1980s, I became acquainted with owners Steve and Bob Buich and with Steve's son Mike, who with Steve now owns the restaurant. (Steve and Bob are brothers; their forebears acquired the restaurant, then almost eighty years old, in 1928.) If I happened to be in the place when business was quiet (generally only from three until five in the afternoon), there would be time to talk with the Buiches about the city hall assassinations, the earthquake, the Giants, or the history of the restaurant. One such afternoon, about six years ago, the Buiches and I were perusing the names of celebrities in the restaurant's guest register. I said something to the effect that someone should write a history of the place. As I recall, Steve Buich then poured me another glass of wine. In short order, I felt like an actor in a slapstick film about army life, when volunteers are called for and everyone takes a decisive step backward—everyone else, that is.

So I have tried to write the story, the biography, of this wonderful old restaurant. And I have tried to write it as Robert Hass, the poet, suggested I do it, entwining its story with San Francisco's. As I found out, that's hard not to do. When San Francisco was scarcely twenty years old, one of France's greatest writers wrote of it as the second-greatest restaurant city in the world. How did that happen in San Francisco—in coarse, adulterous, murderous, gold rush San Francisco? And how could one of the very earliest of San Francisco's restaurants, with such modest beginnings, survive to the present? That's the story I've tried to tell.

The Tadich turned 150 years old in 1999, the year after Rules, London's oldest restaurant, turned 200 years old and Berghoff's, Chicago's oldest, turned 100. The following year, the Tadich could claim that it had served San Franciscans over the course of three centuries and two millennia. Not bad for a joint that began by serving coffee under a tent.

Chapter I

THE RESTAURANT:
Humble Beginnings . . .
in a Tent

"No history . . . of the city, could be complete, unless it included some account of the circumstances which preceded and immediately accompanied its rise, and which have made it what it almost already is, but which it will more plainly soon become, the greatest and most magnificent, wealthy and powerful maritime city in the Pacific—a city which is destined, one day, to be, in riches, grandeur and influence, like Tyre or Carthage of the olden time, or like Liverpool or New York of modern days."

—FRANK SOULÉ, JOHN H. GIHON, AND JAMES NISBET,
THE ANNALS OF SAN FRANCISCO, 1855

San Francisco in 1849, scarcely yet even a town, tottered half inebriate on the brink between the hamlet it had been and the great cosmopolitan city it was about to become. The early predictions of greatness by the authors of *The Annals of San Francisco* would all come to pass in good time. But in one field the city attained greatness surpassingly fast. That field was food. Within a mere twenty years, San Francisco would boast an international cuisine that would rival the great cities of Europe.

In that year of 1849, three Croatian immigrants opened a small eating establishment in San Francisco, calling it, modestly, Coffee Stand. A hundred and fifty-three years later, that restaurant still stands as Tadich Grill.

Since 1849, San Francisco has come to be known as one of the world's great gustatory cities, currently having more restaurants per capita than any other city in the world, about one for every 250 or 300 residents. Its residents and visitors demand as much of their food as any Parisian or Tuscan. Restaurants serving

The Discovery of San Francisco Bay

San Francisco Bay was "discovered" by men under the Spanish captain Gaspar de Portola in November of 1769, just seven years before the little pueblo that became San Francisco was founded on the bay's shore. Portola's men observed the bay from the crest of the Coast Range east of Half Moon Bay, just south of San Francisco. They and Portola himself were distressed to find their route from Monterey to their destination, Point Reyes, obstructed by such a large body of water. Like an alchemist annoyed at having manufactured diamonds, Portola was uncomprehending of the magnitude of the discovery his men had made.

Portola called the bay San Francisco because he thought it was the bay that the Portuguese sailor Sebastián Rodríguez Cermeño had discovered, and so named, nearly two hundred years before, in 1595. But most historians contend that the bay Cermeño had named San Francisco is what we now call Drake's Bay, which lies substantially north of the Golden Gate, in the lee of Point Reyes. That bay is named Drake's Bay because it is widely thought to be the inlet where Sir Francis Drake, the dashing English seafarer, spent the winter of 1579. But some historians say that the bay where Drake wintered in 1579 was actually what we today call San Francisco Bay. On such grounds as this, San Franciscans may be excused their daftness.

opulent continental cookery and self-laudatory "California cuisine" come and go in San Francisco. The Tadich, though, has remained. It has not only survived its and its city's tribulations but has thrived with them, while forgoing fashions such as petty portions and foreshadowing others such as the fetish for freshness. The Tadich represents the quintessence of old San Francisco cuisine.

The three Croatian immigrants who in 1849 opened the Coffee Stand that became Tadich Grill were Nikola Budrovich, Frano Kosta, and Antonio Gasparich. Their business was located in a small, tentlike structure on Long Wharf, also called Central Wharf. The bay has long since been filled in on either side of Long Wharf, and the once-submerged land where the wharf stood is now Commercial Street in San Francisco's financial district. The Coffee Stand owners served merchants and sailors on shore leave from the square-rigged vessels docked in Yerba Buena harbor.

Far less numerous than other ethnic immigrants, Croatians might be said to have had a disproportionate effect on San Francisco's culinary tradition. For one, they introduced San Franciscans to the taste of fish grilled over wood coals. A tradition of the Adriatic seacoast villages of Croatia, this was a novelty in early San Francisco. For another, Croatians have played principal roles in the city's restaurant history. Two of San Francisco's six restaurants that were

The Russians Did Come

Captain Portola, traveling in the company of Father Junipero Serra, was seeking to found a mission in honor of St. Francis of Assisi. Portola was in the service of the Spanish Minister of the Indies, Jose de Gálvez. Gálvez's purpose in colonizing Alta California was to thwart Russian colonization there.

It happens that the Russians weren't there at all. But Gálvez proved the popular saying about paranoia. ("Just because you're paranoid doesn't mean they're not out to get you.") Forty-three years later, in 1812, the Russians established Fort Ross, fewer than a hundred miles north of San Francisco, right asquat the California coast.

At all events, history records that, just as Balboa and not Cortez (as Keats had it[1]) discovered the Pacific Ocean, Portola, and not Drake or Cermeño, discovered San Francisco Bay. The local Native Americans, the Coast Miwoks and the Costanoans, must have been blind to the bay.

founded in the nineteenth century are owned today by Croatian Americans—Tadich Grill and Sam's Grill. (What would have been a third, Mayes Oyster House, was for much of its history owned by the Millisch family, also Croatian Americans. It closed its doors in December 2001.)

Precisely what the menu consisted of when the Coffee Stand first opened, we don't know. Chilean sea bass, Norwegian salmon, and English sole, all flown in by jet now, certainly weren't available. Nor were chicken eggs. Chicken farming hadn't begun in San Francisco or the Bay Area, and eggs could scarcely survive the voyage around Cape Horn. Murre eggs were plentiful, though, as were local oysters, sole, rockfish, salmon, crab, sturgeon, and wild game. As for the customers of this new establishment, they were all non-regulars at first, of course. San Francisco was growing from a village of several hundred into a city of several hundred thousand. The customers included some of these new residents, but many other patrons in 1849 were just passing through, having decided their luck might be better in the gold fields than in this riotous, raucous, fire-prone sprawling new burg.

An Englishman visiting San Francisco in May of 1851 wrote a vivid, if today politically incorrect, description of Long Wharf, or Central Wharf, one that gives a glimpse of the city San Francisco was in those early years:

The Central Wharf of San Francisco, which is nearly a mile in length, is for some distances occupied on either side by Jew slopsellers; and, as these indefatigable gentlemen insist all over the world upon exposing their wares outside their shops, the first glance down Central Wharf impresses you with the idea that the inhabitants of the district have hung their clothes out to dry after a shower of rain. Scattered among the Jew shops are markets for vegetables and poultry, fishmongers, candy-sellers (the Long Wharfers are very fond of sugar-plums), gambling-houses of the worst repute, and drinking-shops innumerable. Being narrow and crowded, and full of loaded drays, drunken sailors, empty packing cases, runaway horses, rotten cabbages, excited steam-boat runners, stinking fish, Chinese porters, gaping strangers, and large holes in the planks, through which you may perceive the water, it is best to be careful in walking down Long Wharf, and to turn neither to the right nor to the left.

The busy street terminates on the city front; and from thence the wharf, which extends for half a mile into the sea, is flanked on either side by ships discharging their cargoes with great order and rapidity.[2]

Parker's San Francisco Directory for 1852 bears out the Englishman's description, listing "drinking saloons," liquor dealers, and tobacconists among the tenants of Central Wharf, which had been renamed Commercial Street in 1851. It listed Number 27 as a "coffee stand" operated by Messrs. "Bennett,

■ The fifth of six San Francisco fires from 1849 to 1851, this one on May 3 and 4, 1851.

Williams, and Gaspar." Nicholas Bennett, Frank Williams, and Anto Gaspar
were the anglicized names taken by Nikola Budrovich, Frano Kosta, and
Antonio Gasparich. Number 27 Commercial Street is between Davis and
Drumm Streets today.

This was, incidentally, an era of fires in San Francisco. Most people today
know only about the "great fire" of 1906. In this period, however, the "great
fire" was the fifth of six fires to eviscerate the city during an eighteen-month
interval that straddled California's admission to statehood (September 9, 1850).
The six fires between Christmas Eve 1849 and June 22, 1851, destroyed about
three thousand structures having a value then of about thirty million dollars.[3]
The phoenix, the mythical bird of ancient Egypt that lived for five hundred
years and, after being consumed by fire in an act of self-destruction, rose from
its own ashes, became part of San Francisco's self-consciousness long before
the earthquake and fire of 1906.

■ Leidesdorff Street, 1879.
Tadich Grill and its
predecessors were located
on or at Leidesdorff Street
for 100 years.

Commercial and Leidesdorff Streets

Commercial Street was an "early—and at that time, an important—business street which ran from the stores and financial houses down to the wharves and piers along Kearny Street."4

Leidesdorff Street is named for William A. Leidesdorff, a black man who was born in the Danish West Indies and raised by a wealthy plantation owner. In 1841, Leidesdorff arrived in San Francisco and became one of its most enter-prising and public-spirited citizens. A merchant and owner of much land, Leidesdorff served as captain of the port of San Francisco. He built the first hotel—the City Hotel—and was appointed vice consul at Yerba Buena in 1845, when California was still under Mexican rule. He also served as city treasurer, a member of the school board, and one of the first municipal council members, as well as, for a time, the Russian consul. Leidesdorff skippered the first steamer on the bay—the Russian ship *Sitka*.5

In 1853, the city's "reclamation" projects (San Franciscans, like the Dutch, were expanding into the sea) forced the Coffee Stand's owners to relocate to the New World Market, the central produce market of the city, located on Commercial and Leidesdorff Streets.

With consummate originality, the three owners of the Coffee Stand renamed their thriving business the New World Coffee Stand. They remained together through 1855, when Budrovich and Kosta sold their interests to Marko Millinovich, making Gasparich and Millinovich partners. Then came a succession of other Croatian American partner-owners—Petar Radovich, Andro Calovich, Gabriel Kustodia, John Franetta—and all the while the restaurant remained in the New World Market.

A 1925 account tells the story a bit differently, with several apparent inaccuracies:

> A talk with Mr. Tadich [John Tadich, who began working at the restaurant in 1876 and later bought it] is like turning back the leaves of historical San Francisco; he can tell you of the little tent, operating on the *northwest* corner of Leidesdorff and Commercial Streets, *prior to 1849,* where coffee was served to sailors and their kind; of a certain Captain Leidesdorff, who docked his ship at this point, with its cargo of iron from Bellhouse & Co. of Manchester, England, and whose crew deserted to go to the gold mines; of the small coffee house tent being transformed by this cargo into a corrugated iron house, which stood in this spot until Mr. Tadich, *in 1882,* turned it into a real restaurant.[6] [Italics added.]

John Tadich did not buy the restaurant until 1887, so we know the 1882 date is incorrect. City records also show that the restaurant had been located at the northeast corner of Leidesdorff and Commercial Streets. Finally, it is unlikely that the coffee house in a tent predated 1849. There simply were too few customers until the gold rush. It's certainly possible, on the other hand, that the iron from Leidesdorff's cargo was used to give the coffee stand real walls. John Tadich became known for his sharp mind and memory, as well as his integrity. The errors in this account are likely the interviewer's, not Tadich's.

We know little about the New World Coffee Stand in the years immediately following 1853 except that it survived and prospered sufficiently that it could move again when it had to, in 1871. In those eighteen years, the gold rush was followed by the silver boom. The Civil War was fought. The Emancipation Proclamation was issued. Lincoln delivered history's greatest utterance of oratory at the dedication of a national cemetery at Gettysburg, and he was assassinated. The years during which the restaurant was housed at the New World Market were eventful ones in the New World.

The great Hayward Earthquake of October 21, 1868, devastated San Francisco and did significant damage to the area of the New World Market. Three years later, the New World Coffee Stand moved to 624 Kearny Street, near Commercial Street, leaving behind the corrugated iron structure built with Leidesdorff's iron. Gabriel Kustodia was now the sole owner, having bought out his partner John Franetta in 1869. The restaurant changed its name ever so slightly to the New World Coffee Saloon, retaining the identity of its former location in the New World Market. (In the latter half of the nineteenth century, San Francisco had scores of coffee saloons, unpretentious eating establishments that served meals, alcoholic beverages, and coffee. They were not unlike today's cafes.)

Little is known, alas, about the owners of the restaurant during this time, such as Franetta and Kustodia, except that they were Croatian immigrants who didn't keep journals—none that we know of anyway. A later Croatian American owner, John Tadich, proved, however, to be a bit of a writer and, although English was not his first language, an eloquent English writer at that. He would reach San Francisco in 1871, as a sixteen-year-old boy.

The First Great San Francisco Earthquake?

The 1868 quake is often described as the first of San Francisco's great earthquakes. However, that is not the case, even if one excludes seismic events that occurred before the arrival of Europeans. The first powerful earthquake to occur in California after the arrival of the missionaries, for example, happened on June 10, 1836. It opened fissures from San Pablo to Mission San Jose, which it destroyed. Only a paucity of population kept this temblor from attaining the infamy of its 1906 and 1989 counterparts. Other earthquakes had also been recorded before 1868, including ones in 1857 and 1865.

Kearny Street

Kearny Street is named not, as many San Franciscans think, for Denis Kearney, the teetotaling Irishman from County Cork who became, in the 1870s, the so-called "Agitator Extraordinary." (The Chinese were the object of his agitation.) Rather, the man for whom the street is named, who spelled his name the way the street's name is spelled, was General Stephen W. Kearny, the American military governor in Monterey just after the Mexican War and before California's statehood. As governor, Kearny appointed Edwin Bryant and George Hyde, in succession, as *alcaldes* of San Francisco (the term "mayor" not having been accepted yet by San Franciscans). Bryant served for only a month, and Hyde just a little longer, but each, like Kearny, got a street named after him.[7]

Chapter 2

THE CITY:
Early Days—Gold and Food

"After Paris, the city with the most restaurants is San Francisco. It has restaurants from every country, even China."

—ALEXANDRE DUMAS *(PÈRE),* 1873

At the time of the French Revolution, when the great French chefs of the day were fleeing the households of their guillotined employers and opening what became known as "restaurants," Europeans—Spaniards, mostly—were just beginning to settle California. Spain founded twenty-one missions in California in the late eighteenth and early nineteenth centuries. Later, the Mexican governor of California made some six hundred private land grants known as "ranchos." Together, the missions and ranchos brought to California a culinary tradition that overwhelmed the dietary habits of the native Californians. In short order, the Spanish and Mexican culinary tradition was itself nearly overrun by the stampeding immigrations of the gold rush. After Sam Brannan shouted news of the discovery of gold, tens of thousands of people from all ethnic backgrounds came to San Francisco seemingly overnight—or within months anyway—many to stay. San Franciscans of Italian, Irish, Jewish, French, and Chinese ancestry are perhaps the most numerous descendants of these early immigrants. Each, even the Irish, has left its mark on San Francisco's culinary palate.

The Tadich, although it has been in the hands of Croatian Americans since its beginnings in 1849, and though it touts itself as a fish house, has hardly been impervious to the many other ethnic influences in San Francisco, particularly the early ones. A typical menu today lists, in addition to grilled fish, minestrone, Boston clam chowder, cioppino, bouillabaisse, boiled beef tongue with Creole sauce, shrimp or seafood curry, and Camembert cheese. No "early" California dishes, such as tamales, appear on the menu.

Much of San Francisco's pre–gold rush cuisine survived the mid-nineteenth-century immigrant hordes to California and persists to this day. The cuisine did not consist of tacos and fajitas and flautas, though it was surprisingly not far from these. Early California food, *los comidas California de antes*, was a mixture of Mexican and Native American fare. The first Spanish settlements, the missions, established to convert the "heathen" California natives to Christianity, introduced the natives to Spanish and Mexican food, and the natives in turn shared local seeds, nuts, berries, game, and fish with the Spanish priests, or *padres* (fathers). Early California food became a simple cuisine based on corn, beans, rice, meat, poultry, and fish. Corn was ground into masa, a meal, and made into tortillas. Where wheat grew better than corn, wheat-flour tortillas were made. The principal dishes were *frijoles* (beans), *arroz* (rice), *enchiladas*, and *tamales*, all of which are still to be found in today's Mexican restaurants in California. An early California feast is described in a classic novel of the period, *Ramona* by Helen Hunt Jackson:

> At last supper was ready—a great dish of spiced beef and cabbage in the centre of the table; a tureen of thick soup, with forcemeat balls and red peppers in it; two red earthen platters heaped, one with the boiled rice and onions, the other with the delicious *frijoles* (beans) so dear to all Mexican hearts; cut-glass dishes filled with hot stewed pears, or preserved quinces, or grape jelly; plates of frosted cakes of various sorts; and a steaming silver teakettle, from which went up an aroma of tea such as had never been bought or sold in all California.[1]

Hangtown Fry

The story of the Hangtown Fry is that, during the gold rush, a condemned prisoner at Hangtown in the mother lode country ordered for his ritual last meal an omelet made with fried fresh oysters. (The Sierra Nevada town is now more pleasantly named Placerville.) Oysters, then as now, weren't found in abundance in Hangtown. How long the condemned man prolonged his execution—indeed, whether he escaped it entirely as a consequence of his request—is still the subject of research and conjecture. (Some have theorized, with substantial plausibility, that the condemned man's request for a dish with eggs was more effective in prolonging his execution, so much rarer were eggs than oysters.) Hangtown Fry persists today in many variations in many restaurants. Tadich's version tastes unlike what you'll find at Sam's, the Fly Trap, or any of the dozens of other places where it is found on the menu.

■ The Presidio of San Francisco, founded in 1776.

San Francisco in the middle years of the nineteenth century grew as perhaps no other city in the world has grown. Until 1849, the agglomeration of three settlements that became San Francisco amounted to little more than a hamlet or village—and a sleepy one at that. A census taken of San Francisco in the summer of 1847 (the year the pueblo of Yerba Buena, now in American hands, changed its name to San Francisco), recorded a population of 469. It counted all of 157 houses in the village, most of them one-room wooden cabins.[2] By 1849, however, the year Tadich Grill was founded, the population had grown forty-fold, to 20,000, and the City of San Francisco was becoming

The Three Settlements of San Francisco

The first settlement in San Francisco was the Presidio. Established by the Spanish rulers of California on September 17, 1776, the Presidio was a military garrison near the southern entrance to the Golden Gate.

The second settlement was the Spanish mission that every San Franciscan calls Mission Dolores. It still stands in the eponymous Mission District, at Dolores and 16th Streets. Franciscan priests led by Father Francisco Palou, an associate of Father Junipero Serra, founded Mission Dolores a few weeks after the Presidio was established, on November 9, 1776. The mission's real name is Mission San Francisco de Asis (for St. Francis of Assisi). Why it is called Mission Dolores (Mission Sorrows) baffles many San Franciscans. There was once a small lake nearby named Laguna de los Dolores (Lake of the Sorrows), and folks apparently started calling the mission after the lake instead of the saint.

The third settlement was the little pueblo of Yerba Buena. An Englishman, William Richardson, founded the pueblo in 1835 on the present site of Portsmouth Square, a community park in Chinatown bounded by Kearny, Grant, Clay, and Jackson Streets. Its name is taken from the U.S.S. *Portsmouth*,

■ Mission Dolores, founded in 1776 and now the oldest building still standing in San Francisco.

an American naval vessel captained by John B. Montgomery that sailed into San Francisco Bay in July 1846, during the Mexican-American War that resulted in the American annexation of California.

known throughout the world.[3] As the population rose meteorically, so also did San Francisco's fame as a city of restaurants.

There was a reason the city's population was swelling so in 1849. Gold had been discovered on January 24 of the previous year in the tailrace of Captain John Sutter's sawmill at Coloma, east of Sacramento. When the news reached San Francisco in March, the San Francisco newspaper *The Californian* reported the story in a brief paragraph on the back page. Two weeks later, the editor of the rival weekly, hard-drinking Sam Brannan of the *California Star*, who had visited the mill and met with Sutter, wrote that reports of the

---

The Eggers

David "Doc" Robinson came to California from Maine to join the gold rush, not as a miner but as a burlesque actor with no theater. Once in San Francisco, Robinson rented a whale boat with his brother-in-law Orrin Dormann and set sail for the Farallon Islands, twenty-seven miles west of the Golden Gate. There he plucked thousands of eggs from the rocky nests of that large, black, lumbering seabird, the California murre (*Uria aalge californica*). He lost half the eggs in a squall on the return voyage but still netted three thousand dollars. With that nest egg, Robinson was able to open his theater, the Dramatic Museum.

Robinson thus hatched and fledged his theatrical career, while word spread of the mother lode he had found on the Farallons. That word began a period of plundering that soon turned into a fully fledged egg war, replete with shootouts and murder. Undoubtedly the largest casualty, though, was the murre population itself. The wholesale robbery of murre eggs had, by the turn of the century, nearly destroyed the Farallon Island murres.

Until the rise of the Petaluma chicken-farming industry in the 1880s, murre eggs were served in San Francisco restaurants. They were uniformly described as tasty. Southeast Farallon Island was the destination of the "eggers" of the nineteenth century. The landing there, then as now, was rough, and lives were lost in the attempt. The eggers clambered up and over cliffs where, one writer wrote, "goats would hesitate." The egging season began in late May and ended in July, during which time tens of thousands of murres gathered on the craggy, precipitous cliffs to breed. Murre eggs, colored in shades of cream, pale blue, or green, with brown mottling, are pear-shaped, tapering toward one end. When jarred loose from their nest, they tend to roll in a tight circle rather than sliding off the steep ledges on which the nests are built.

strike were "a humbug." It was no small irony, then, that Brannan, having himself returned from the diggings (and perhaps having first made a few advantageous business deals), strutted down Montgomery Street in mid-May of 1848, brandishing a vial filled with nuggets and shouting, "Gold!"[4] Brannan is generally credited as the man who awakened the sleepy village, and all the world beyond, to the discovery in the Sierra Nevada of that metal. After that, to borrow the title of Jim Holliday's book, the world rushed in.

The gold rush transformed California. As a historical event, it is probably fair to say that its sweep and scope are not fully comprehensible even today. For 150 years, writers, social commentators, and historians have tried to wrest from words some sense of the force of the gold rush. The historian Jim Holliday wrote, in his wonderful *The World Rushed In*, "Everything about California would change. In one astonishing year the place would be transformed from obscurity to world prominence. . . . The impact of that new California would be profound on the nation it had so recently joined."[5] Novelist Wallace Stegner called the gold rush a

■ Samuel Brannan, 1819–1889.

"universal mass trespass that shortly created laws to legitimate itself."[6] One of the most remarkable characterizations of it was written during the first flushes of the gold rush. In an article published in early 1850, Karl Marx and Friedrich Engels predicted that the gold rush "will have much greater consequences than the discovery of America itself."

The gold rush transformed San Francisco as well. Robert Louis Stevenson described the city's transformation in an obscure essay:

> Within the memory of persons not yet old, a mariner might have steered into these narrows (not yet the Golden Gate), opened out the surface of the bay—here girt with hills, there lying broad to the horizon—and beheld a scene as empty of the presence, as pure form the handiworks of man, as in the days of our old sea commander. A Spanish mission, fort, and church. . . . Now, a generation later, a great city covers the sandhills of the west, a growing town lies along the muddy shallows of the east; steamboats pant continually between them from before sunrise till the small hours of the morning; lines of great seagoing ships lie ranged at anchor; colors fly upon the islands; and from all around, the hum of corporate life, of beaten bells, and steam, and running carriages, goes cheerily abroad in the sunshine. . . . Nothing remains of the days of Drake but the faithful trade-wind scattering the smoke, the fogs that will begin to muster about sundown, and the fine bulk of Tamalpais looking down on San Francisco, like Arthur's Seat on Edinburg.
>   Thus in the course of a generation only, this city and its suburbs have arisen.[7]

Stevenson wrote about San Francisco's eating establishments, too: "You taste the food of all nations in the various restaurants. . . ." He wrote of French, German, Italian, and Chinese restaurants but omitted the many restaurants run by immigrants from Croatia.

Soon after the discovery of gold, San Francisco attained a culinary distinction to match its financial renown. The story of San Francisco's rise to financial fame—the rise of its gold, silver, railroad, and banking barons—has been often told. The story of its culinary ascendance is less well known but no less remarkable. As the population grew, there arose the "eating-houses, of which there was an immense number in every portion of the town," according to San Francisco's 1855 chroniclers, Soulé, Gihon, and Nisbet. "These were of every description, good, bad, and indifferent." Within twenty years

■ Daguerreotype circa 1850, reputedly the oldest known photograph of San Francisco. Looking east from the corner of Clay and Kearny.

Marx and Engels on the Gold Rush

"Now we come to California. The most important thing which has happened here, still more important than the February revolution, is the discovery of the California gold mines. Even now, after scarcely eighteen months, it can be predicted that the discovery will have much greater consequences than the discovery of America itself. . . . A coastline which stretches across thirty degrees of latitude, one of the most beautiful and fertile in the world, is now being visibly transformed into a rich, civilized land thickly populated by men of all races, from the Yankee to the Chinese, from the Negro to the Indian Malay, from the Creole and Mestizo to the European. California gold is pouring in torrents over America and the Asiatic coast of the Pacific is drawing the reluctant barbarian peoples into the world trade, into the civilized world. For the second time world trade has found a new direction. . . . Then the Pacific Ocean will perform the same role as the Atlantic does now and the Mediterranean did in antiquity and the Middle Ages—the great sea-route for international traffic—and the Atlantic Ocean will decline to a mere inland lake, such as the Mediterranean is today."[8]

of the onset of the gold rush, San Francisco had established itself as a city of gastronomic notoriety. In an 1873 book, the great French writer Alexandre Dumas wrote, "After Paris, the city with the most restaurants is San Francisco. It has restaurants from every country, even China." How did that meteoric culinary rise happen?

San Francisco's financial fortunes were in large measure the seed bed for its gastronomic good fortune, for good cooks have always come dear. Fortunes were made first from the California gold fields and then from the Nevada Comstock silver discovery ten years later. In the 1860s, four Sacramento merchants, Collis P. Huntington, Charles Crocker, Mark Hopkins, and Leland Stanford, formed the Central Pacific Railroad Company (later the Southern Pacific). This company built the western portion of the Transcontinental Railroad. After the railroad's completion at Promontory Point, Utah, in May 1869, the "Big Four," as they came to be known, rose to be among the wealthiest men in the world.[9] Another lucrative partnership was the Bank of California, formed in 1861 by William C. Ralston and Darius Ogden Mills, which became one of the mightiest banking institutions in the country.[10]

Financial fortunes alone, however, didn't account for San Francisco's swift rise to greatness in the gastronomic world. Men outnumbered women in

---

San Francisco's Earliest Restaurants

According to the 1855 account by Soulé, Gihon, and Nisbet, "There were the American *dining-rooms,* the English *lunch-houses,* the French *cabarets,* the Spanish *fondas,* the German *wirthchafts,* the Italian *osterie,* the Chinese *chow-chows,* and so on to the end of a very long chapter. There were cooks, too, from every country; American, English, French, German, Dutch, Chinese, Chileno, Kanaka, Italian, Peruvian, Mexican, Negro, and what not. Hence people of any nation might have choice of a place of the kind, kept by their own countrymen, and where dishes were served in styles to suit their accustomed and peculiar appetites and fancies. There was an endless variety, too, in the character of the provisions furnished; for besides the common products of the country, importations were constantly arriving from all sections of the globe. Of game no other market ever furnished so great an abundance or so general an assortment."[11]

Alexandre Dumas, Food Writer

Dumas's remark about the "city with the most restaurants" was included in his *Le Grand Dictionnaire de Cuisine,* published in 1873, three years after the author of *The Three Musketeers* and *The Count of Monte Cristo* had died. Which may lead one to ask whether the author of *Le Grand Dictionnaire* was not Alexandre Dumas *(père)* [father], but rather his illegitimate son of the same name, commonly referred to as Dumas *(fils)* [son], who himself attained a degree of renown for his novels and plays. As it happens, the father had completed *Le Grand Dictionnaire* the year of his death and had the manuscript delivered to his publisher in March 1870, but the outbreak of the Franco-Prussian War delayed the book's publication.[12] I have found no evidence, incidentally, that Dumas ever visited San Francisco.

Some have considered the *Dictionnaire* Dumas's greatest achievement. The caption beneath a sketch of Dumas in Katherine Bitting's *Gastronomic Bibliography* reads, "A noted author and gourmand who wrote novels and stories because he needed the revenue but produced his masterpiece, the "Grand Dictionnaire de Cuisine," because he loved the work."[13]

It is perhaps surprising, given his prolific literary output throughout his life, that Dumas waited until so near the end to submit the manuscript for publication. It may have been that, unlike the case of his other writings, he wrote it himself and did not make use of his legions of ghostwriters. Once, upon meeting his son and namesake, Dumas asked, "Have you read my latest novel yet?" Dumas *fils* replied, "No, have you?"[14]

San Francisco for many years. That meant few traditional households and a consequent demand for private cooks and restaurants (not to mention other institutions of pleasure). In 1868, Noah Brooks, a writer for Bret Harte's new *Overland Monthly* (and an old friend of the assassinated Abraham Lincoln), wrote about these single men, and other San Francisco restaurant customers, for the principal benefit of the magazine's eastern audience:

> But the single men are not the only customers to [San Francisco's] restaurants. Not a few childless couples live in lodgings, and have their food brought to them by servants from the eating-houses, in that advanced stage of staleness which justifies the epithet of "cold victuals."[15]

Nature too was a factor in San Francisco's growing culinary greatness. The city was surrounded by game forests; a bountiful sea; farms and ranches producing meats, fowl, and produce in abundance; and soon the best wineries in the country. Brooks explained, "Our perennial season of fruit and flowers, our wealth of game and profusion of rich meats, are not at all suggestive of the frugal or substantial dinners of the older states of the Union."[16]

The raucous arrival of Mary Ellen "Mammy" Pleasant provides an early illustration of San Francisco's hunger for fine food. When the mysterious, famous, and later infamous southern cook, a black woman, reached the city in the 1850s, there was such demand for her services that she auctioned them off; the high bid was five hundred dollars a month. During her life in San Francisco, she cooked for several bachelors' clubs and for Governor and United States Senator Milton Latham.

But Mammy Pleasant was not long alone as a master cook in San Francisco. Eastern capitalists came west to survey their investments, and when they did they brought with them their French chefs, who, like the ship hands of the vessels of the forty-niners, often did not report for the voyage home. These chefs found quick work in San Francisco, both from the rich and the not-so-rich. The millionaire François Pioche, who had resided in San Francisco since before the gold rush, brought forty chefs from Paris to slake, and stoke, the city's ravenous appetite for French cuisine.[17] And when San Francis-

Mammy Pleasant

Mammy Pleasant figured in more than just San Francisco's culinary history. In 1883, Senator William Sharon of Nevada, eight years after his wife had died and to all appearances an unmarried man, was arrested in San Francisco on charges of adultery. The accuser was his mistress, Sarah Hill. The court cases arising from the arrest went on for nearly ten years, providing salacious reading in the San Francisco papers.

The mysterious, wealthy, and powerful Mammy Pleasant, a reputed voodoo queen as well as an extraordinary cook, was a confidante of Hill's and a principal witness in the case.[18]

Mammy Pleasant was also the confidante of many other powerful and wealthy San Franciscans. She arranged assignations and contrived to control the fortunes of others. A short alley on Nob Hill, near Grace Cathedral, is named for her.

cans returned from traveling abroad, they brought back tastes, and recipes, acquired in their travels.

French chefs followed the forty-niners to San Francisco. And Creole, Peruvian, Spanish, Chinese, and Croatian chefs came as well, all finding in San Francisco an extraordinary natural bounty of fish, game, and fruits and people with money to spend on fine food. Small wonder the city got off to such a good start food-wise.

Chapter 3

THE RESTAURANT:
Growth and the Cold Day

". . . my heart is like melting spring snow on the mountain."

—John Tadich

"It's a cold day when I get left."

—Alexander Badlam Jr., regular patron and
soon-to-be-deposed San Francisco assessor, 1882

In 1871, the year the New World Coffee Saloon moved to Kearny Street, a sixteen-year-old immigrant named John Tadich arrived in San Francisco from Dalmatia on the Adriatic coast of Croatia.

Why Tadich made his voyage is not difficult to comprehend. For a thousand years, since the Slavic peoples who called themselves Croats first settled in the old Roman province of Dalmatia, their land had been a prize and a pawn of the great powers. Among the incessant invaders were the Venetians, Turks, and Austrians (several times each), Mongols, and French. Political upheaval was incessant as well.

John Tadich was born in Starigrad on the island of Hvar. According to his own moving essay in the book *The Slavonic Pioneers of California,* he felt a great melancholy on leaving his native Dalmatia and his parents, Vincent and Katherine Tadich:

■ John Tadich.

> On the twenty-second day of May, in the year 1871, I left my native town of Starigrad, in Dalmatia, on the beautiful eastern coast of the Adriatic Sea. It was a day not to be forgotten, the birds were singing and the flowers were in full bloom, and I, about to depart for the promised land, "zlatna California," the golden California, was happy beyond all description. Relations and neighbors came to wish me good luck, and God speed. But when it came to parting from my dear mother, I lost for the time being the picture of beautiful California. Even now, after all these years, I can remember clearly her parting words: "Sinko moj, s Bogom, cuvaj, svoj zivot, i moli Boga za svoje zdravlje, i nemoj zaboraviti, Deset Zapovjedi Bozjih," which means in English: "My son, God be with you, take care of yourself, pray God for your health, and do not forget the Ten Commandments of God."
>
> While I am writing these lines and thinking about my dear mother, my heart is like melting spring snow on the mountain.[1]

Tadich's trip to America took him to Split, Trieste, Vienna, and Berlin. "That [stop in Berlin] gave us an opportunity see a wonderful sight—the treat of a lifetime," he wrote more than fifty years later. The sight was "train after train loaded with soldiers returning from Paris, jubilant and with smiling faces, rejoicing over the victorious outcome of the Franco-Prussian War of 1870." Berlin was a stopover on the way to Hamburg,

> which was at that time, as it is now, a very important seaport of great commerce. From Hamburg we took the steamer across the channel to Leeds, England. From Leeds, we went to Glasgow, Scotland by train at sixty miles an hour—some speed. We stayed at Glasgow for two days or so until our ship was ready to leave for New York.

With several more adventures, the young John Tadich made it to America, and from New York he traveled by railroad through Chicago, Burlington, and Council Bluffs.

> To my young mind, it was a wonderful trip, filled with much pleasure. I shall never forget the beautiful scenery and I am happy that I had the opportunity to

see the country as it was then. I can never see again those wonderful sights under the same conditions, and I feel it was a great privilege to have traveled from Omaha through Nebraska, Wyoming, Utah, Nevada and on to California in those days. The immense plains, the majestic Rocky MMountains [sic], the picturesque Sierra Nevada mountains and the romantic valleys of the beautiful golden state of California, the numerous Indians in their primitive costumes, are always before me.

I recall now that whenever our train would stop on a side track, hudreds [sic] of Indians and their squaws, with papooses on their backs, would gather around the train. They were just as curious about us as we were about them. Another interesting thing to me was my first sight of a group of Chinese. They were little men, with almond-shaped eyes. They had on large sun hats and were repairing the railroad bed. The sight of Indians and the Chinese made a lasting impression and I enjoy the recollection to this day.[2]

After this adventure, recorded so articulately, John Tadich arrived at the San Francisco home of his uncle Nikola Buja on July 22, 1871. He worked at Buja's Coffee & Liquor Saloon at 605 Davis Street for two years, and then at Peter Chiucovich's Wine & Liquor Saloon at the southeast corner of Pacific and Sansome Streets. In 1876, he became employed as a barkeeper at the New World Coffee Saloon.

The years following John Tadich's arrival in San Francisco in 1871 were eventful ones in San Francisco, no less than the previous eighteen years had been. On Saturday, August 2, 1873, Andrew Hallidie successfully descended the Clay Street hill in San Francisco's (and the world's, for that matter) first cable car. It was also during this time that Golden Gate Park, first decreed

Dalmatia and Croatia

Dalmatia, during the latter days of the Roman Empire in the fourth century, was the name given to the portion of the Balkan Peninsula now occupied by the countries of Slovenia, Croatia, Bosnia and Herzegovina, Yugoslavia, and part of Albania. Today the name Dalmatia applies only to the region of Croatia along the Adriatic coast.

Croatia takes its name from the Croat people. They were Slavs who in the seventh or eighth century immigrated to that land from the marshy flatlands north of the Carpathian Mountains, in what is now Ukraine, a thousand miles away.

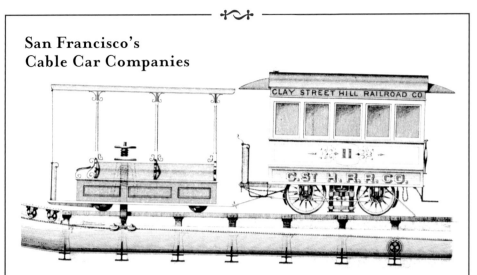

San Francisco's Cable Car Companies

■ Andrew Hallidie's prospectus for the world's first cable car, 1873.

While only three cable car lines run in San Francisco today, in the sixteen years following Hallidie's first successful run, San Francisco spawned eight cable car companies that operated six hundred cars over one hundred miles of track. Oakland, Los Angeles, Chicago, New York, St. Louis, London, and Sydney were among other cities later to build cable car lines.

by the state legislature in 1870, sprang into being under the inventiveness of William Hammond Hall, its first architect, and later John McLaren.[3]

Three years after John Tadich first went to work for the New World Coffee Saloon, the restaurant outgrew its Kearny Street quarters, and in 1879 it moved to larger premises at 221 Leidesdorff Street, between Commercial and Clay Streets. It continued to call itself the New World Coffee Saloon (there were still many coffee saloons in San Francisco in those days), though it had been eight years since it had been in the New World Market. It was a nice coincidence that the restaurant had again landed on Leidesdorff Street, considering that Leidesdorff's iron cargo may have enabled the restaurant to progress from a tent to a building in the first place. In 1880, John Tadich left the restaurant to become bartender at Nathan Cook's Liquors on Ellis Street.[4] But he returned to work at the New World Coffee Saloon two years later. In another five years, this young immigrant, who would become a pillar of San Francisco's business and Slavic communities, would own the place.

An essay on John Tadich appears in the 1932 publication *The Slavonic Pioneers of California.* The author, J. L. Kerpan, writes,

> At the risk of offending his innate modesty, the writer can state, without the fear of contradiction, that today Mr. Tadich is the most widely known and most highly respected member of our San Francisco colony. As one who does not seek either praise or glory, Mr. Tadich seems to be entirely unaware of that fact, but the writer feels sure that all those who know Mr. Tadich, and their name is legion, will subscribe to this statement without qualification. And that achievement alone makes life worth living.[5]

■ Alexander Badlam Jr.

In 1882, Alexander Badlam Jr., San Francisco's arrogant tax assessor, ran for reelection. Badlam, the nephew of California's first millionaire,[6] Sam Brannan, took as his reelection campaign slogan, "It's a cold day when I get left." In the idiom of the day, the slogan meant that it would be a rare day when he would be left without a victory at the ballot box. This infuriated his opposition and irked the voters of San Francisco as well, who overwhelmingly voted Badlam out of the office he had held for eight years. The boisterous assessor, who with his high-rolling cronies was a habitué of the New World Coffee Saloon, sought refuge there after his defeat. In 1925, John Tadich recalled the story:

> On the corner of Stockton and Geary there used to stand the old "Wigwam," the headquarters of the Republican party, many of whom were regular patrons of Tadich's Grill [not yet so known, of course]. Alexander Badlam, running on the Regular Republican ticket for assessor, at his nomination spoke the words which were later to become famous: "I thank you, gentlemen," he said, and then added: "It is a cold day when I get left."
>
> But when election came, it was a cold day for Badlam, for John Seibe, the Independent-Republican, was elected. [In point of fact, Badlam was defeated by Louis F. Holtz.]
>
> Practical jokers literally impressed the cold day on Mr. Badlam, by running huge slabs of ice into his domicile, the night after election, wrapped in horse blankets. The defeated candidate and his friends sought consolation at Tadich's (when consolation could be administered in liquid form), and from that time on, the place was known as "The Cold Day Restaurant."[7]

This incident, along with the severely cold weather that November of 1882, supplied the newspapers with ample material to lambaste Badlam for weeks. Without his uncle Sam Brannan's provocative promotion, the gold rush might not have happened so precipitately. And had it not, Tadich Grill might not have been established. And without the braggadocio of Brannan's nephew Badlam, the place, for all we know, might still be known as the New World Coffee Saloon.

In 1882, the year of the "cold day" incident, the restaurant was owned by Samuel Becir and Eugene Masounette. The following year, the two took as a partner Gaspar Pavica, who in short order acquired Becir's interest. In 1887, John Tadich, who had worked at the restaurant since 1876, bought Masounette's interest in the establishment. Pavica remained a partner for perhaps a year, but Tadich bought him out in 1888 and remained the sole owner until 1905, when he very briefly took Rafo Dumarac as a partner. Dumarac was Tadich's second-to-last partner; their partnership ended in the devastation of San Francisco that occurred the following year.

■ Looking down Sacramento Street from Powell Street during the 1906 fires.

A little after five o'clock the morning of April 18, 1906, one of the most violent earthquakes in recorded history convulsed San Francisco. Had there been a Richter scale, the quake would have measured about 8.3, according to modern estimates. (The Richter scale is logarithmic; an 8.3 quake releases roughly 75 times the energy of a 7.0 tremor like the 1989 San Francisco quake, according to Jack Moéhle, professor of seismic engineering at the University of California at Berkeley.) The tremors lasted more than a minute, which, as anyone who has felt a serious earthquake can attest, must have seemed like an extended eternity. At the epicenter of the quake, in Olema just north of San Francisco, the part of the earth west of the San Andreas fault moved twenty feet to the north. Today, remnants of fences still reveal the offset.

In San Francisco, when the pitching and shuddering subsided, fires broke out throughout the city as ruptured gas mains ignited. Water mains had ruptured too, and with the city's firefighters thus nearly helpless, the fires raged for four days. The last was extinguished on April 22 at the corner of Francisco and Montgomery Streets, near North Point.[8]

The 1906 earthquake and fire felled or incinerated most of the city, including The Cold Day Restaurant. They likewise destroyed the nearby Adriatic Restaurant, which was owned by John Sutich, another Croatian American. When the smoldering had stopped and the bulk of the rubble had

Quakes and Fires

With the exploding population of San Francisco, occasioned by the gold rush, earthquakes had been put out of mind, in large part because of the frequency of fires. The fires caused San Franciscans to rethink their building practices, and so wood-frame construction gave way to brick and other masonry.

However, masonry, as it happens, collapses in earthquakes to roughly the same degree that wood is consumed in fire. The 1865 quake prompted Mark Twain to write an "Earthquake Almanac" in the *San Francisco Dramatic Chronicle*. One entry was, "Occasional shakes, followed by light showers of bricks and plastering. About this time expect more earthquakes, but do not look out for them, on account of the bricks."[9]

Bret Harte was asked why Oakland was always spared the destruction earthquakes wreaked on San Francisco. Citing "Schwapplefurt, the celebrated German geologist," Harte suggested there are some things the earth cannot swallow.[10]

John Tadich Reminisces

John Tadich, in his short memoir, is vague in describing his personal life after arriving in San Francisco in 1871:

After being here many years after my arrival in 1871, I spent considerable time "going around and seeing things" in compliance with the advice of my good friend, Jakov Mikulich, and eventually I returned to Europe where I remained for nearly nine months. [Just when this was he doesn't tell us, but it was prior to his purchase of the Cold Day in 1887.] There I married the girl of my choice, Antoinette Ivanisevich, a daughter of the well-known Ivanisevich family of Stari-grad. I returned to San Francisco with my bride, and we had three children, a son, Danilo, and two daughters, Mabel and Ruby. Danilo is married and is associated with the Shell Oil Company; Mabel is a teacher in the San Francisco Public School Department; Ruby is married and is now Mrs. Herbert F. Suhr. She has a little son, Herbert F. Suhr Jr.[11]

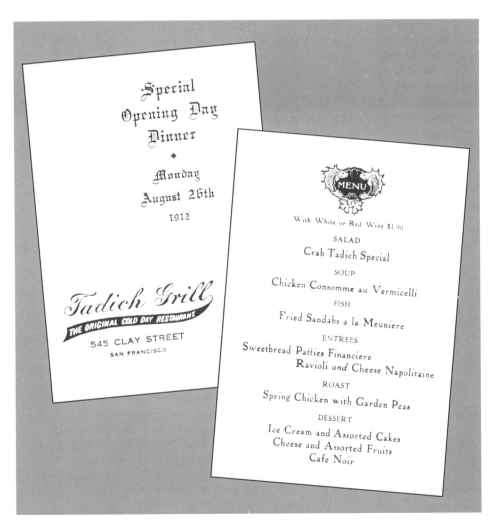

■ Cover and interior of Tadich's reopening menu on August 26, 1912.

been carted off, Tadich and Sutich temporarily set up a combined business at 417 Pine Street, calling it by Tadich's restaurant's name, The Cold Day Restaurant. A year later, the two moved their joint restaurant to number 441 of the same street and block, where it remained until 1912, when the six-year partnership of Tadich and Sutich broke up. Tadich then established himself at 545 Clay Street, at Leidesdorff (once again). Sutich remained at 441 Pine and appropriated the name The Cold Day Restaurant. Tadich was mightily annoyed by this perfidy of his six-year partner (the temperate Tadich, according to his daughter Ruby, was incapable of any form of anger greater than annoyance). Tadich then modified the name of his restaurant to Tadich Grill, The Original Cold Day Restaurant, the name still used today. His reopening at 545 Clay Street took place on August 26, 1912.

In 1997, at the age of ninety-three, John Tadich's daughter Ruby recalled the time of this incident:

> When my father was out of the Sutich partnership, he became very upset, distraught. But our household was maintained the same. Our living was maintained the same, and my father spent much more time gardening.[12] He had the most beautiful dahlias. They were show dahlias. He tended to his garden, he had his garden clothes, and we had a room, like a maid's room downstairs, where he kept his gardening clothes, and changed into and out of them. He was very meticulous, always. Everything was fastidious in his life, orderly and fastidious.[13]

Like the operators of many other San Francisco enterprises (including the builders of the Golden Gate Bridge[14]), Mr. Tadich turned for financial help to A. P. Giannini, the legendary founder of the Bank of America. As Ruby Tadich recollects:

> When he went back into business by himself [in 1912], because A. P. Giannini and he were boyhood friends, he went to him. A. P. said to my father, "You can have anything you want. Just write checks. You have that amount of money." And that's how he went back into business.

Five years after the 1912 breakup, on December 7, 1917, John Tadich's estranged partner Sutich was shot in an apparent robbery attempt in the

■ 545 Clay Street, home to Tadich Grill from 1912 to 1967.

vestibule of his home at 1576 Waller Street.[15] It was initially thought that Sutich would die from his wound, but he was only blinded, and lived another forty years. He kept his restaurant and took a partner, Carl Dubac, to run the business, which by that time had moved to 537 Sacramento Street. They maintained the restaurant until 1940. Dubac died the following year, and Sutich died in 1958.

In the meantime, the future of Tadich Grill—its next ninety years at least—was being set in motion. John Tadich continued to burnish the restaurant's reputation for good food and honest dealings. In 1913, the year after he reopened as Tadich Grill, he hired as a pantryman a young Croatian immigrant named Tom Buich. Fifteen years later, a Buich would buy the restaurant from Tadich, and the family has owned it ever since.

Chapter 4

THE CITY:
From Boom to War

"Nowhere in the world, perhaps, is there so great a variety of comestibles as in these restaurants."

—NOAH BROOKS, 1868

Noah Brooks's 1868 article on San Francisco's restaurants appeared in the November issue of Bret Harte's new *Overland Monthly*, which enjoyed wide circulation in the East. "The restaurants of San Francisco," he wrote, "are numerous, plenteous, inviting and even cheap." The French chefs in San Francisco, accustomed to making "ambrosial banquets from nothing," had initially grown "quite demoralized" at the "astonishing luxuriance of the raw material for Titanic feasts":

> For six months in the year strawberries are common, and at all seasons there is an abundance of fresh fruits of some sort. Grapes and pears that grace only the tables of the very wealthy in Atlantic cities, are lavished here in unstinted profusion. Reed-birds, quail and wild ducks in their season, and domestic fowls, are almost as common as beef-steaks and chops in other lands.

The influences on San Francisco cuisine were as varied as the city's ethnic makeup. The cuisine has "contributions of nature and art . . . from every land beneath the sun," Brooks wrote. "Russian caviar, Italian macaroni, German pretzels, Swiss cheese, Yankee codfish-balls, English roast beef, Spanish omelets, French kickshaws and Mexican ollas and Asiatic nameless things, all blend in the banquet which San Francisco restaurants daily set before their thousands of captious, hungry and exacting guests."[1]

In the latter half of the nineteenth century, five restaurants that have survived to the present, in addition to Tadich Grill, opened in San Francisco. They were the Cliff House, the Old Clam House, Sam's Grill, Fior d'Italia, and Schroeder's. (What would have been a sixth, Jack's, closed just before Christmas 2000, a victim of rocketing real-estate values. Jack's reopened in a different guise in 2002. Mayes Oyster House on Polk Street closed in December 2001; it would have been a seventh.) They are all among the oldest restaurants in the United States.

The Cliff House at Land's End (1090 Point Lobos Avenue), which first opened in 1858 (or 1850 or 1863, depending on the source), has suffered three fires that completely or virtually destroyed the restaurant. (The fires occurred in 1887, 1894, and 1907. The great San Francisco fire of 1906, which followed the earthquake, did not reach Land's End and in fact did not extend west of Van Ness Avenue.) Each time, the restaurant was rebuilt at the original site.

Some Other Older Restaurants in America

Bookbinder's, Philadelphia's oldest restaurant, began operating in 1865, making it decidedly younger than Tadich Grill (and three other San Francisco restaurants as well). It is located at 125 Walnut Street, on Society Hill. Chicago's oldest, Berghoff's on Adams Street between State and Dearborn, celebrated its centennial in 1998.

The oldest restaurant in our nation's capital may be the Old Ebbitt Grill, which was founded in 1856. No other restaurant seems to claim the title. But the Old Ebbitt was founded in 1856 as a tavern, and its current owners are careful to tout it not as Washington's oldest restaurant but as its oldest *saloon*. (That is the case with what might otherwise be New York's oldest restaurant as well.) The Old Ebbitt is currently located at 675 15th Street, N.W.

■ The Cliff House
  in 1905.

The fourth and present Cliff House was built in 1909. It was bought in 1939 by George K. Whitney (a frequent diner at Tadich Grill), who operated it for many years.[2]

The Cliff House was not one of San Francisco's fanciest restaurants. But with the exception of a period of mediocre cuisine and management in the 1960s and early 1970s (when one could find it, with its spectacular views and roaring fire, virtually empty on a Saturday at sundown), it has long been a San Francisco favorite. Clarence Edwords wrote in 1914,

> Lovers of the night life know it well for it is the destination of many an automobile party. But for a most pleasant visit to the Cliff House one should choose the early morning hours, and go out when the air is blowing free and fresh from the sea, the waves cresting with amber under the magic touch of the easterly sun. Select a table next to one of the western windows and order a breakfast that is served here better than any place we have tried. This breakfast

will consist of broiled breast of young turkey, served with broiled Virginia ham with a side dish of corn fritters. When you sit down to this after a brisk ride out through Golden Gate Park, you have the great sauce, appetite, and with a pot of steaming coffee. . . . Of course there are many other good things to order if you like, but we have discovered nothing that makes so complete a breakfast as this.[3]

The Old Clam House, at the corner of Oakdale and Bayshore, has been in its present location since it was founded, as the Oakdale Bar & Clam House, in 1861. Little is known about the origins of the Clam House except that an early proprietor was one C. Yaeger and that it was spared when the 1906 fire was stopped at 20th Street, some distance north of the restaurant. The reference to Yaeger is provided by no less an authority than the Ancient and Honorable Order of E Clampus Vitus, Yerba Buena Chapter, which has affixed a plaque to the outside wall of the restaurant.

Jack's on Sacramento Street between Kearny and Montgomery, opened in 1864, but as was mentioned closed at the end of 2000. Like the Cliff House and Old Clam House, it had been at the same address all its years. (Jack's reopened in 2002, revived by Philippe Jeanty.) Sam's on Bush Street opened in

■ The Old Clam House, formerly known as the Oakdale Bar & Clam House.

1867, and Fior d'Italia, which appears to have vindicated its claim as the oldest Italian restaurant in the United States, opened in 1886. The Fior is presently located at the southwest corner of Union and Stockton Streets. Schroeder's on Front Street has served German food since it opened in 1893.

In her wonderful book *Old San Francisco*, Doris Muscatine writes of Mayes Oyster House, Sam's Grill, and the old California Market,

The California Market was one of the best places to obtain seafood, housing under its giant canopy such emporiums as Darbee and Immel's, M. B. Moraghan [renamed Sam's Grill in the 1920s], the Pearl Oyster House, and Morgan's, where a typical two-bit meal consisted of a great mound of shellfish, a good small steak, and a mug of steaming coffee. Mayes Oyster House, still run by a crew of Yugoslavs, keeps on the current menu, besides Hangtown Fry, another early specialty, the oyster loaf. Consisting of a hollowed loaf of toasted French bread filled with plump fried oysters, the loaf earned an early reputation for being so good that it could calm the wrath of any spouse when brought home by an erring husband. Sam's Grill . . . specializes in cooking fish in its present location on Bush Street. In the early days its most popular dishes were breaded turtle steak and green turtle soup, and the proprietors continued to import live deep-sea turtles well into the 1930s.[4]

By the latter years of the nineteenth century, San Francisco was thought of as another Paris, a bit coarser but nearly as enlightened in gastronomy, and unsurpassed in decadence. The city boasted superb French restaurants. One was the Poodle Dog (a miners' corruption, happily embraced by the city and the restaurant's owners, of Poulet d'Or, "golden chicken"), with its great chef George Brauer, later of Blanco's. Others were Delmonico's, St. Germain,

Norton I

Joshua Norton arrived in San Francisco in 1849 and soon made a fortune in real-estate speculation. A few years later he sought to corner the world rice market, but he failed and lost his fortune in 1854. He disappeared for a few months, but one day re-appeared, striding down Montgomery Street in a uniform that mixed Army and Navy regalia, replete with flying epaulets. He carried a gnarled grapevine cane and wore a feathered beaver cap. At the offices of the *San Francisco Bulletin,* he placed an announcement proclaiming himself the Emperor of the United States and Protector of Mexico.

Accompanied on occasion by two dogs, Bummer and Lazarus, Emperor Norton lived another twenty-six years, always appearing in the same attire. In 1869, standing atop Rincon Hill (the western anchorage of the Bay Bridge today), he decreed the bridging of San Francisco Bay. (Norton's bridge, however, was to have continued from San Francisco to "the mountain range of Sacilletto" and thence to the Farallon Islands, some twenty-seven miles out to sea.) Norton's imperial exchequer, a printer on Leidesdorff Street, supplied the Emperor with cash certificates in ten-, twenty-five-, and fifty-cent denominations. These were accepted in all the restaurants and bars of San Francisco, which saw to it that Bummer and Lazarus were also well fed.

Historians have never decided whether Joshua Norton grew truly demented after his rice speculation failed or just more shrewd.

The Yerba Buena Chapter of E Clampus Vitus dedicated a plaque to Emperor Norton at the entrance to the Cliff House in the 1930s. From the Cliff House at Land's End on a fogless day, one can make out the Farallon Islands, the western anchorage of Norton's bridge.

The Clampers effected an exchange with the

■ Norton I, Emperor of the United States and Protector of Mexico.

ownership of the Cliff House a few years ago. In the Norton plaque's place is an uncharacteristically sober slab of metal honoring Adolph Sutro, who built the first Cliff House. The Clampers's original plaque has been recast and redated and is found now in the little redwood grove next to the Transamerica Pyramid.

Maison Riche, Marchand's, the Pup (at Stockton and Market, owned by Old Pierre, who had been a thrifty waiter at the Poodle Dog[5]), and Maison Dorée. Their sauces and soufflés were, to judge by contemporaneous accounts, the equal of the restaurants of Paris.

These restaurants helped bring about the establishment of another San Francisco institution—the discreet, private upstairs dining room. Upstairs dining rooms were outfitted with locked doors, ample couches, and a street entrance well separated from the restaurant's main entrance. Vestigial if not

---

The Ancient and Honorable Order of E Clampus Vitus

Sir Francis Drake was an early member of E Clampus Vitus, as any knowledgeable "Clamper" will tell you, and it is difficult to refute the claim since, the organization keeps no records. Magellan and Erasmus too were Clampers. In truth, E Clampus Vitus was founded by a forty-niner from Missouri named Joe Zumwalt. The Ancient and Honorable Order spread in the early 1850s from its origins in the mining communities to San Francisco, Nevada, and as far south as San Diego. As its faux Latin name suggests, it was begun as a parody of the established fraternal organizations such as the Masons and the Oddfellows. Its constitution contains the fundamental principle that all members are officers and all officers are of equal indignity. Its rituals are resplendent with monstrous props (for example, the Staff of Life, which must be grasped), and nonsensical incantations that could have been, and might have been, written by Samuel Clemens. Its chief officer is the Noble Grand Humbug. It meets in the Hall of Comparative Ovations.

The creed of the ancient order is *Credo quia absurdum,* real Latin that means "I believe because it is absurd." Its motto, also in Latin, is *Per caritate viduaribus orphanibusque, sed prime viduaribus,* which translates literally as, "Through charity toward widows and orphans, but primarily toward widows."

The world headquarters of E Clampus Vitus today seems to be Murphys, California, though no one, least of all the Noble Grand Humbug, is at all sure. A primary purpose of the latter-day ancient order is the erecting of monuments and affixing of plaques commemorating arcane pieces of California history. One such plaque is attached to the wall of the Old Clam House. Another was long affixed to the south entrance to the Cliff House; it paid homage to Norton I, Emperor of the United States and Protector of Mexico, and his dogs, Bummer and Lazarus.

Les Cabinets Particuliers

Henry Bruen introduced private rooms—*cabinets particuliers*—into San Francisco's French restaurants in 1851. Many of the restaurants that featured these rooms had two entrances, one for the family or for traditional get-togethers, the other for private assignations. The typical dinner at one of San Francisco's early French restaurants consisted of between twelve and eighteen courses and untold quantities of liquor and wine, and lasted perhaps six hours. As Doris Muscatine has written, following such a meal "it was a wonder if any participant could do anything more dangerous than fall into a long, heavy stupor."[6] Regardless, these restaurants provided all the accoutrements and amenities necessary for the tryst. In addition to couches, door locks, and a communication system of buzzers and velvet pulls, there was the quintessential element: a cadre of the most discreet waiters. It was not unusual for diners to spend the night.

vestal remains of such facilities, of interest perhaps only to anthropologists, were to be found above the now-defunct Amelio's Restaurant on Powell Street, and on the long-unused third floor of Jack's. An early chronicler wrote of the Poodle Dog that "numerous convivial parties of men and women found its private rooms convenient for rendezvous."[7] At Delmonico's on O'Farrell Street, "carriages drove directly into the building from the street and the occupants went by elevator to soundproof rooms above, where they were served by discreet waiters."[8] Several of the equally discreet waiters at the old Jack's on Sacramento Street, who were laid off when the restaurant was sold and closed for renovation at the end of 1996, spent a Sunday morning before the closure videotaping the place, and the upstairs rooms in particular, reminiscing on the audio track about what had gone on up there. The tape is encased in a year 2500 time capsule, or it is unpurchasable at any price, except perhaps a great one. The story varies.

The greatest of the San Francisco restaurants of the late nineteenth century may have been the dining room at the Palace Hotel. In recent years, the hotel has been called the Sheraton Palace Hotel. The unnecessary first word is as offensive to San Franciscans as "Frisco" is, and new owners have, happily, dropped it. When he built the hotel in the 1870s, then the largest in the world, silver baron William Ralston was equally put off by the last word, preferring that the establishment be known simply as the Palace.

■ Entrance to the Palace Hotel's
central court, circa 1850.

The dining room at the Palace, from its beginning, was one of the great
restaurants of the world and one of the most prolific as well. A New York
theatrical troupe in 1876, shortly after the hotel opened, embarked on a public-
ity stunt: It closed its New York run and took off by rail across the continent,
breaking all land speed records, to open in San Francisco. The train made it
faster than planned and the troupe showed up early for a Palace Hotel breakfast. They were served Salmon Grille à la Maître d'Hôtel, Tom Cod Frit with
Sauce Tartare, Cucumber Salad, Filet de Boeuf with Sauce Béarnaise,

Côtelettes d'Agneau with Sauce Soubise, Escalope de Veau à la Guennoise, Pomme de Terre Maître d'Hôtel, Rognon Sautés au Champignon, Poulet Grillé au Cresson, Oeufs Brouillés aux Points d'Asperges, Oeufs Frites au Temben, Pet Salé, Omelettes au Rhum, and apricots, raspberries, strawberries, and cherries.[9]

The Palace was severely damaged in the 1906 earthquake. It was rebuilt, and resumed playing host to and serving the world's elite. The mid-twentieth century, though, saw it become a shabby specter of its former self. In the late 1980s, it was treated to a transforming face-lift, making it once again one of the more opulent hotels in San Francisco. Brass, brilliant panes of leaded

---

Billy Ralston and the Palace

William C. Ralston, rightly called the Builder of San Francisco, and Darius Ogden Mills formed the Bank of California in San Francisco and established branches in Nevada, where silver had been struck. The bank's manager there was William Sharon, later a United States senator. Sharon established an interest rate of 2 percent per month instead of the prevailing 3 to 5 percent, and he rarely refused a borrower. In short order, the bank had lent 3.5 million dollars and had foreclosed on most of the silver mills in Nevada. Through 1865 and into the next year, the outlook was dark. But then Sharon and Ralston hit upon a device to keep their heads above water. With Mills and two other bank officers, they organized the Union Mill and Mining Company to operate the mills that the bank had taken possession of, and through the bank they pressured the mines to deliver their richest ore to these mills. The scheme worked, for a while.

On August 26, 1875, Sharon sold all his stock in these mines, causing speculation that the mines had paid out. This, in turn, caused a run on the Bank of California, which was forced to close its doors the next day. The bank's auditors determined that Ralston owed the bank five million dollars. Ralston was forced to sign over his assets to Sharon, and was summarily fired. Ralston then walked to North Beach for his customary daily swim and, by accident or design, he drowned.

Ralston didn't live to see the opening of his Palace Hotel, for more than thirty years the largest in the world. It opened October 3, 1875, a little more than a month after his death, the same day that Sharon reopened the Bank of California. In that short time, Sharon had acquired much of Ralston's property, including the hotel.[10]

glass in the the main dining room, the Garden Court; elaborately turned newel posts and balusters; plush rugs and carpeting; and a vast, restored, breathtaking *Pied Piper* by Maxfield Parrish embellish the refurbished hotel. The kitchen of the Garden Court is markedly improved over what it had been for too many years.

Dickey's Road House, on Fulton Street near Fifth Avenue, just across from Golden Gate Park, was a favorite Sunday breakfast joint in the late 1800s, presided over by Colonel Dickey himself. "Dickey's, particularly on Sunday mornings, was the rendezvous of the *bon vivants*," as Evelyn Wells has one of her characters, the Judge, report in *Champagne Days of San Francisco*. "I saw a man once . . . breakfasting in Dickey's—solely on absinthe and olives! . . . Never again, epicures assure us, will steaks be seen such as Dickey's."[11]

London's Oldest Restaurant, and the Prince's *Cabinet*

In London, Rules rules. Located on Maiden Lane in London's theater district, Rules is the oldest restaurant in a city with two thousand years more history than San Francisco. It was founded in 1798, just fifty-one years before Tadich Grill. It celebrated its two hundredth birthday in 1998 and soon afterward celebrated having served customers in the course of four centuries.

Ricky McMenemy, Rules's general manager, proudly points out its upstairs Charles Dickens Room and, across from it, the Edward VII Room. Dickens met, ate, drank, and conversed with friends in his eponymous room.

Meetings of a different sort occurred in the room named for Edward.

(Edward was scorned by his mother, Queen Victoria, until her death. She blamed her son for the death of her beloved husband, Albert, Edward's father, who one cold and rainy night went searching for the young, wayward prince among the seamier districts of London and thereupon caught his death of cold.) Edward, explains McMenemy, met in the Rules room named for him with his lady friend, Lillie Langtry, the great actress who first appeared in San Francisco in 1884. When I pointed out to Mr. McMenemy that Ms. Langtry ultimately retired in Northern California and there planted a vineyard and built a winery, that the winery is still producing quite good wines, and that they were missing from the wine list at Rules, McMenemy promptly promised to add them.

San Franciscans near the end of that century, unlike current city residents, were as owlish as South Americans are today. (One of Evelyn Wells's characters boasts he never rose before four in the afternoon.) Zinkand's on Market Street, which served German food, and the Midway Plaisance were favorites of the late after-theater crowd. Oysters were a staple at the Midway, whether eastern or local, in many sizes and served raw, fried, steamed, stewed, roasted, or baked eleven different ways. Served with a chilled Château d'Yquem, oysters were also featured at many other restaurants, including Goodfellow's Grotto in the Civic Center and Gobey's Ladies and Gents Oyster Parlor on Sutter Street. Another favorite place for oysters was the California Market, with its many restaurants and bars.

Atop Telegraph Hill, perched like an eagle's aerie, was the Castle, which one got to by cable car. Not a cable car as we know it, but one suspended beneath a cable, strung from the toe to the crest of the hill. The Castle lasted but a few years, burning just before the 1906 earthquake.

Pre-earthquake San Francisco boasted many excellent Italian restaurants, among them the Buon Gusto, La Estrella, Campi's, La Gianduja, and the Fior d'Italia. An early chronicler of San Francisco's restaurants wrote of the Fior:

We went to that restaurant for dinner one evening, and the proprietor, knowing our interest in human nature studies, showed us to a little table in the back part of the room, where we could have a good view of all the tables. Our table was large enough to seat four comfortably, and presently, as the room became crowded, the proprietor, with many excuses, asked if he could seat two gentlemen with us. They were upper class Italians, exceedingly polite, and apologized profusely for intruding upon us. In a few minutes another gentleman entered and our companions at once began frantic gesticulations and called him to our table, where room was made and another cover laid. Again and again this occurred until finally at a table suited for four, nine of us were eating, laughing, and talking together, we being taken into the comradeship without question. When it came time for us to depart the entire seven rose and stood, bowing as we passed from the restaurant.[13]

The Hoffman Grill, on the south side of Market Street between Second and New Montgomery Streets, was another long-lived San Francisco eating establishment founded during this era. (The structure, but not the restaurant, was saved when, in the 1980s, an office building was constructed on its east, south, west, and top sides.) Nearly ninety years ago, in his *Bohemian San Francisco*, Clarence Edwords wrote, "To speak of Bohemian San Francisco and say nothing of the old Hoffman saloon, on Second and Market streets, would be like the play of Hamlet with Hamlet left out." Presided over by "Pop" Sullivan, it had "the most magnificent bar in San Francisco, and in connection was a restaurant that catered to people who not only knew good things but ordered them."[14]

New Orleans's Old Restaurants

Antoine's, founded in 1840, is New Orleans's oldest restaurant. Another great and elder New Orleans restaurant, and one with ties of friendship to Tadich Grill's Buich family, is Commander's Palace. It was built in 1880, not by some military officer but by one Emile Commander. Since 1969, it has been owned by Ella and Dick Brennan, the younger sister and brother of Owen Brennan, who with his father founded New Orleans's famed Brennan's Restaurant in 1946. (The older brother died in 1955, scarcely forty-five years old.) As a young woman, Ella's daughter Ti Martin, who now runs Commander's Palace, worked for a brief spell with chef John Canepa in the Tadich kitchen.

There were Mexican as well as Spanish restaurants in pre-earthquake San Francisco. Spain gave Mexican cooking the tamale, and Mexico gave Mexican cooking the tortilla. Clarence Edwords wrote that the tamale "had its origin in Spain and was carried to Mexico by the conquistadors, and taken up as a national dish by the natives after many years. The tortilla, on the other hand, is made now exactly as it was made by the Mexican Indian when the Spanish found the country."[15]

The best of the best Mexican restaurants was Luna's, on Vallejo and Dupont (now Grant) Streets. The dishes were characteristically early California, "from the unpalatable soup (Mexicans do not understand how to make good soup) to the 'dulce' served at the close of the meal," Clarence Edwords wrote. "Mexican restaurants of the present day in San Francisco are a delusion, and unsatisfactory."[16] Nevertheless, at Luna's "of a foggy evening you might see Joaquin Miller or Frank Norris; and you would always find Ricardo, the sashed and mustachioed one-eyed waiter, who ran the show."[17]

Among the Bohemian restaurants in pre-earthquake San Francisco were the Fly Trap (now reincarnated on Folsom near Second), the St. Germain, and Jules', all of which "gave their customers eight courses and a bottle of wine for half a dollar."[18] Others were Steve Sanguinette's, Luchetti's, and the vastly popular Papa Coppa's.

Papa Coppa's specialty was chicken in a coconut, which set back the customer a dollar six bits. Giuseppe Coppa, who had trained at a number of the city's better restaurants, including the Poodle Dog, stewed a disjointed chicken in peppers, corn, onions, and a sauce inside a sealed coconut shell.

But Papa Coppa's great popularity stemmed more from his generosity than his culinary virtuosity; he was wantonly liberal with his artist clientele. The coterie of writers who met frequently at Papa Coppa's restaurant during the early years of the twentieth century, just before the earthquake and fire, included Jack London, Wallace and Will Irwin, short-story writer James Hopper, and the aging Ambrose Bierce and his two brilliant pupils, the poets Herman Scheffauer and George Sterling, later named poet laureate of California.

A few years before the earthquake, Papa Coppa had the restaurant repainted, and it was done badly. His artist friends and customers decided to redo the repainting, gratis, and the project was undertaken by just about all of the artists in the city. The resulting joint mural took three months to complete.[19]

Unfortunately, the magnificent murals were to last but a few years; they were destroyed in the earthquake and fire of 1906. Coppa afterward opened a succession of establishments, many as lavishly painted as his first, but none had the same magic. He did not retire until the late 1930s, but his greatest moment may have been in the days of cooling ash just after the quake. Then, with some of his friends, he dug out the remains of his old joint and, "there amid the ruins, he served dinner to his patrons, and what a dinner it was!"[20]

All the best restaurants of the day perished in the fires following the 1906 earthquake, and most were never to reopen. Among those that did not were Marchand's, a favorite of Sarah Bernhardt; the Maison Riche at the corner of Geary and Grant; the Maison Dorée, famous for its oysters and frog legs; Delmonico's; the Pup; and the Poodle Dog.

■ Girard's French Restaurant, 65 Ellis Street.

The years after the earthquake in San Francisco were nothing short of astounding. The city rebuilt itself, celebrated with a lavish world's fair, went to war, endured Prohibition, built during the depths of the Great Depression three of the engineering wonders of the world (two bridges and the Hetch Hetchy waterworks), held a second, arguably more lavish, world's fair, and went to war again.

After the earthquake, the Louvre, on the corner of Fillmore and Ellis Streets, was the first restaurant of consequence to open. It was followed soon after by Techau's Tavern at 15 Powell Street (near the cable car turntable today). Tait's, another notable post-quake restaurant, was run by Carl Zinkand; he had been the proprietor of a pre-quake establishment that bore his name.

The best French fare in post-earthquake San Francisco was found at Felix's on Montgomery Street, the Poodle Dog-Bergez-Frank's on Bush Street, and Girard's French Restaurant on Ellis Street. Girard's chef had, before the earthquake, worked for twenty years with the great Victor Hertzler at the St. Francis Hotel. Girard's well-known French dressing was first offered for public sale in the 1930s and is still marketed today, though doubtless using a quite different recipe from the original. Other restaurants were Pierre's on Pine Street and La Favorite on Pacific Street.

John's Grill and Bardelli's narrowly missed being three-century restaurants. Each opened in the years just after 1906. John's on Ellis Street, of *The Maltese Falcon* fame, opened in 1908. Bardelli's on O'Farrell Street opened the following year. John's, now owned by John Konstin, is doing fine and has been for many years. Bardelli's, though, suffered the indignity of a several-fold increase in rent in 1997 and was forced to close its doors.

Blanco's was one of San Francisco's favorite and most extravagant restaurants in the years after the earthquake. Antoine de Bua Blanco (for whom Edward Blanquie of Jack's was often mistaken) opened it in 1907. Blanco had owned the Poodle Dog restaurant when the fire destroyed it. When he started up his new enterprise, he brought along with him George Brauer, who had for many years been his head chef at the Poodle Dog. Blanco's offered lavish musical entertainment and some of San Francisco's best cuisine in surroundings of extravagant opulence, even by pre-earthquake standards. Venetian glass chandeliers dripped from the ceilings, frescoes and intaglios festooned the walls, and balconies of boxes hung from three sides of the hall. The balconies rested on massive, elaborately decorated columns and were curtained in garnet draperies that could be drawn across for privacy.

Blanco's closed in 1935, during the middle of the Depression. Its premises were taken over by the Music Box Restaurant, which had none of the magic of the old place.

Among the Italian restaurants to rebuild and reopen after the earthquake were Campi's, run by the Campagnolis (a retired Italian opera singer and her musician husband), Fior d'Italia, and Brenti's La Gianduja. La Gianduja was located at the corner of Union and Stockton Streets in the heart of North Beach. (At the same corner today are Fior d'Italia and La Felce, and, half blocks away, Moose's and the North Beach Restaurant.) The Leon d'Oro and New Frank's on Clay Street were also new Italian restaurants that opened after the fire.

The boundary between the theater district and the seamy Tenderloin is not easy to demark today, and it wasn't any easier in the early part of the twentieth century. The Bay City Grill, at Turk and Market Streets, was definitely in the Tenderloin. At the east end of the Tenderloin, or perhaps in the theater district or the Union Square district, was Herbert's Bachelor Grill at 151 Powell Street.

In Dashiell Hammett's *The Maltese Falcon*, detective Sam Spade sleuths through five days in 1928 San Francisco.[21] Many of the city's landmarks are given fictitious names (for example, the St. Francis Hotel is called the St. Mark), but two restaurants are called by their true names. One is Herbert's Bachelor Grill, where Spade eats in chapter 6. The other is John's Grill on Ellis Street. In chapter 17, Spade

> went to John's Grill, asked the waiter to hurry his order of chops, baked potato, and sliced tomatoes, ate hurriedly, and was smoking a cigarette with his coffee when a thick-set youngish man with a plaid cap set askew above pale eyes and a tough cheery face came into the Grill and to his table.
>
> "All set, Mr. Spade. She's full of gas and rearing to go."[22]

John's Grill today has a vast display of *The Maltese Falcon* memorabilia. Herbert's has gone the way of all flesh.

The great *San Francisco Chronicle* columnist Herb Caen defined the Tenderloin as "the 'Terrific Triangle' bounded by Jones, O'Farrell and Market." In 1963, he mused over the name and wrote that "for a comparatively few years as a city's time is reckoned, there was," in the prewar Tenderloin, "more action than anywhere else in the country." He continued,

> Tenderloin: a peculiarly American term, born in New York. The lexicographers aren't too sure about its origin; the most educated guess surmises that the cops on a certain beat in Manhattan were able to afford tenderloin steaks. In San Francisco, the juice was rich enough for filet mignons, sparkling burgundy, apartment houses and places in the country.

In those few years, he wrote,

> There were fine restaurants: the Techau Tavern at 1 Powell, Newman's College Inn, the Bay City Grill, Herbert's Bachelor Grill. There were the "French" places—Blanco's, the St. Germain—with utter respectability on the ground floor, shady booths on the second, "riding academies" (as they were known) on the third.[23]

Izzy Gomez's place on Pacific Street in the Barbary Coast was a favorite Bohemian hangout in the post-quake years. The story—one that the 300-pound Izzy never troubled to refute—was that Gomez had been a Shanghaier. In his *Bohemian San Francisco*, Henry Evans wrote that "the place was noted for its dirt, profanity (which Izzy didn't like), excellent steaks, low-priced drinks and general color. Sunday morning, Teddy (who was bouncer as well as swamper) used to give the place a thorough cleaning. The broken teeth, glass, furniture and discarded garments would make a noticeable pile."[24]

In between wars, while the city managed a second world's fair (a third, if you count the Midwinter Fair of 1894), its restaurants didn't do half badly either. North Beach, always the Italian quarter, briefly was known as the Latin Quarter. Its southern boundary was Broadway, and in the four blocks between Kearny and Powell Streets were Italian restaurants such as the venerable Fior d'Italia and vibrant newcomers such as Amelio's, Vanessi's, and New Joe's, "where crowds wait for seats at three in the morning."[25] Just down Montgomery Street from Broadway was Ernie's.

Ernie Carlesso, who had taken over the Hotel Il Trovatore, opened Ernie's in the 1930s. The restaurant remained in business until 1996. After World War II, it exchanged its sawdust floors, free drinks for GIs, and family-style Italian food for a niche as perhaps San Francisco's most elegant restaurant. In 1963, Herb Caen wrote that Alfred Hitchcock, relaxing in Union Square, was descended on by scores of pigeons. "Kicking at them good-naturedly, the director of *The Birds* admonished, 'Get thee to Ernie's—I'll see you under glass at 7.'"[26]

Amelio's at 1630 Powell Street was founded in 1926 by four Italian men (partner Amelio Pacini drew the long straw). Long a San Francisco favorite, it too closed in 1996.

New Joe's at 536 Broadway, from 1928 until it closed in the early 1970s, was a North Beach mainstay, the originator of the Joe's Special and the progenitor of a prolific line of "Joe's" restaurants, none of which—not even Original Joe's on Taylor Street, which came later—is related to the original. (And never mind that a restaurant near Lefty O'Doul's on Geary Street calls itself New Joe's today. That restaurant was opened by Jeff Pollack in 1984.)

New Joe's began as a card room at the Broadway address, operated by a gambler named Joe Merello, the owner of Club Moderne on Sutter Street. Merello always wore a white hat and, as Herb Caen put it, "a showgirl on each arm." To camouflage his operation, Merello installed a tiny hamburger stand in front of the card room. There were only a few stools and Pete Arrigoni, the cook. Arrigoni's hamburgers, served on hollowed-out loaves of sourdough bread with fried onions, were so good that almost unmanageable crowds thronged the establishment. Soon Arrigoni bought the hamburger stand and card room space from Merello and expanded his new restaurant to include what had been the card room. He then named it New Joe's, to indicate that Joe Merello was no longer around.[27]

Joe's Special is familiar to San Franciscans as a simple concoction of sautéed onions, mushrooms, a bit of garlic, ground beefsteak, chopped spinach, and eggs, all in a scramble. The story goes that bandleader Bunny Burson invented the dish early one morning when he wandered into New Joe's for a meal after his gig. Arrigoni protested that he had only some spinach, ground beef, a few eggs, and, well, you get the idea. Caen, who died February 1, 1997,[28] long maintained the story, as did my long-deceased father, who claimed to have bussed tables there the very night.

Merello, incidentally, later sold his Club Moderne to Tommy Harris, who subsequently opened his long-running Tommy's Joynt, specializing in such dishes as buffalo stew, on Van Ness Avenue.

Half a block from New Joe's was Vanessi's, which opened in 1936. Located at 498 Broadway, it expired at the end of 1988. (Fior d'Italia was for many years sandwiched between the two at 504 Broadway.) Herb Caen wrote in the *San Francisco Chronicle* on January 18, 1989,

> Vanessi's closing came as a slight shock. This place was an institution from the night it opened in 1936. Joe Vanessi, an ex-bootlegger who once ran a speakeasy at 77 Broadway called the Cairo (his real name: Silvio Zorzi), knew everybody in town and everybody went to Vanessi's—politicos, sports people, showbiz stars, socialites. Customers stood three deep for a seat at the counter, to watch the cooks threaten each other with cleavers in mock fights.

Joe Vanessi died in 1971. The day after his funeral, Caen wrote, "He was a wonderful garbler of names. 'Hello, there, Mr. Hoppe! [pronouncing it "Hoppy"] he'd say to Bob Hope. Once he got sued because he refused to serve a black man who turned out to be Paul Robeson: 'Would I have kicked him out if I'd known it was Paul Robinson?' he apologized."[29]

In the North Beach of the years of the Roaring Twenties and the Depression, there were also Mexican, Spanish, and Latin American restaurants—hence, the name Latin Quarter. These places included Xochimilco, Sinaloa, Jai-Alai, and Espanol. And there were other, not decidedly ethnic restaurants, such as Club Lido, Bal Tabarin, Lucca's, and the Fiesta Club, as well as Joe DiMaggio's and Fishermen's Grotto.[30]

Trader Vic's was a restaurant of wantonly undecided ethnic charm. Its founder, Trader Vic Bergeron, brought back from his Far East and South Pacific travels recipes, whole cuisines, and notions and combined them all into his lavish, Polynesian-motif restaurant. The original Trader Vic's, founded in 1936 in Oakland, was called Hinky-Dink's. So many San Franciscans claimed it as theirs that he opened a restaurant in the city in 1951, on little Cosmo

Mary Frances Kennedy Fisher

Assertive and arch, M. F. K. Fisher wrote in the first chapter of her first book, "One of the stupidest things in an earnest but stupid school of culinary thought is that each of the three daily meals should be 'balanced.'"[31]

At once an icon and an iconoclast in matters gastronomic, M. F. K. Fisher lived most of her adult life in Glen Ellen and Napa. She wrote twenty books about food, or ostensibly about food. W. H. Auden called her the best prose writer in America.

Fisher once wrote of her family's visit to San Francisco for the 1915 Panama-Pacific Exposition, when she was a girl of five. "We learned about rex sole—obviously named, in some way, for our father, Rex Kennedy—and about sand dabs. Father said the latter were the most delicate fish in the world, especially as served at Sam's. Mother stood up for rex sole meunière, because of her husband's name and because Uncle Evans had found it at Jack's to be even better than the pompano at Antoine's in New Orleans, wherever that was."[32]

Place, a sprite of an alley near the Bohemian Club. It was shut with scarcely a whimper some time this past decade, after its founder died.

In between wars, the growing California tradition of food writing flourished. It was then that the genius of M. F. K. Fisher first manifested itself in print. The first of her many tracts on food, the capricious and slightly enigmatic *How to Cook a Wolf,* was published in 1942, at the onset of World War II.

In a more conventional voice, Alice B. Toklas wrote an account of her return from Europe to her native San Francisco in the summer of 1934, in the company, of course, of Gertrude Stein:

> We indulged in gastronomic orgies—sand dabs *meuniere,* rainbow trout in aspic, grilled soft-shell crabs, *paupiettes* of roast fillets of pork, eggs Rossini and *tarte Chambord.* The *tarte Chambord* had been a specialty of one of the three great French bakers before the San Francisco fire. To my surprise in Paris no one had ever heard of it.[33]

Great restaurants and great food writers notwithstanding, in the years leading up to World War II, three palls in turn were laid on San Francisco's gastronomic scene. The first was Prohibition. The second was the Great Depression. The third was the war itself. At the war's end, a renaissance of San Francisco's culinary tradition slowly began again.

Chapter 5

THE RESTAURANT:
The Buich Era

"I should let the Buich family have it. They won't disgrace my good name."

—JOHN TADICH

In 1913, the year after he reopened as Tadich Grill, John Tadich hired another Croatian immigrant, Tom Buich, as a pantryman. Tom Buich (Tomo Buic) had left Croatia for the United States in 1907 at age fifteen. He worked for Tadich Grill for five years but was fired in 1918. Tom, an assertive sort, had told Mr. Tadich, how *he* would run the place. To spite Tadich, Tom Buich went to work for John Sutich, the expropriator of the name The Cold Day Restaurant. Five years later, though, in 1923, Tom Buich returned to Tadich Grill as a waiter.

Mitch Buich (Miho Buic), the oldest of the three Buich brothers, entered the employ of John Tadich in 1914. He was born, like his brothers, on a farm in a village outside Dubrovnik, in 1890. At sixteen, he came to the United States and found work in San Francisco at the Potrero Cafe, owned by Chris Kristovich, at 2544 Third Street. After several other restaurant jobs, Mitch Buich went to work for Tadich Grill as a cook, and in 1924 he became the chef.

In 1928, he returned to Croatia to marry Marija Miloslavich. Returning to the United States later that year, he and Louie Milich, a waiter at Tadich Grill, bought the restaurant from John Tadich.

Louie Buich (Luko Buic), the youngest of the three Buich brothers to work at and ultimately own Tadich Grill, was born in 1897. At the age of seventeen, he was drafted into the Austrian army to fight in the First World War. Following the war, he made his way to San Francisco in 1922, where, with the help of his brother Mitch, he got work at Tadich Grill as a dishwasher. Louie worked with Tom at John Sutich's The Cold Day Restaurant for a short while, but returned to the Tadich in 1923 as a cook. Louie met his wife, Marija Nenad, in 1927 in Oakland, though she had been born and raised approximately two miles from Louie's birthplace near Dubrovnik. They married in 1929 and had three children, Mary Lucille, Steve, and Robert. Steve and Robert (Bob) later became owners of the restaurant.

In 1928, after fifty-two years with the restaurant, John Tadich, hospitalized and in ill health, was told by his doctors that he had little time to live. He agonized over his need to sell the restaurant and ultimately sold it to Mitch Buich and Louie Milich for $8,000 ($4,000 apiece). Louie Milich sold his interest five years later to the restaurant's landlords, Hugo Paladini and his sister, Henrietta Paladini Cavallero, for $2,500. The Paladinis, in addition to owning the building at 545 Clay Street where the restaurant was located, also owned the wholesale fish market across the street at 540 Clay Street, which provided the restaurant with much of its seafood, so they had economic reasons for wanting the restaurant to survive. When Mitch Buich couldn't afford to buy out his partner, the Paladinis bought Milich's share, holding it until Mitch's brothers, Tom and Louie, had saved enough to buy their share in 1934 for $3,000 ($1,500 each). The restaurant has been owned by Buiches ever since.

■ Gentleman's souvenir Tadich Grill quill toothpick, circa 1920.

The Buich brothers then became working owners. Mitch was chef. Louie was the night chef and relief day chef. Tom was the "front man," host and bartender.

In a conversation with Steve and Bob Buich, John Tadich's daughter Ruby recalled her father's decision to sell the restaurant, seventy years after the fact:

I will tell you how my father determined to leave the restaurant business. He was in the hospital when he was told how ill he was, and he had this big decision to make. He said, "If I go downtown, and offer my place for sale, I won't get what I should get for it." So he decided on what the price should be. Then he weighed his options between Big Ben and Steve Markovich [other employees who wanted the restaurant] and your family [the Buiches]. And my father couldn't decide which way was fair, because they were all equally good employees. Big Ben was attractive, and my father was very fond of Steve, his cousin. My father had introduced him to Masonry. But Big Ben was a little ostentatious. And in the end my father said, "Well, I think I should let the Buich family have it. They won't disgrace my good name." He had great respect and esteem for the Buich family, and that was his decision.[1]

Having been told at the age of seventy-three that he suffered from a terminal illness, John Tadich also cashed out of the stock market in February of 1929 (eight months before the crash). But his doctors had been wrong. Tadich lived another twenty-four quite healthy years, not dying until late 1953 at the age of ninety-eight.

Shortly after he sold the restaurant to Mitch Buich and Louie Milich, John Tadich stopped in for lunch, still thinking he had little time to live. When he was leaving, he asked Milich for a small bottle of tarragon vinegar to take home, which he fully intended to pay for. Milich muttered some surly remark and Tadich, offended, refused to take the vinegar and refused to return to the restaurant. After Milich sold his interest in 1933, Tom Buich called Tadich and told him the Buich brothers had become the sole owners, and asked him to please return. Tom added, "And you're welcome to take all the tarragon vinegar you want, with our compliments." Tadich welcomed the call, returned to the restaurant many times, and became a close friend of the Buich brothers.

Ruby Tadich remembers visiting the restaurant as a child: "We occasionally took friends to dinner. Maybe once a month. And perhaps Saturday night my mother and I would go, and come home late with father. He had become a millionaire, and none of us in the family knew that. Everything about him was low key. Nothing was ostentatious."

Although she spent little time in it as a child, Ruby Tadich was well aware of one distinguishing fact about the restaurant. Over lunch on April 8, 1997, she asked Bob Buich, "Do you pride yourself on the fact that you were the first restaurant to use the mesquite to grill fish?" Bob responded, "I certainly do," with a smile.[2]

The Prohibition years provided some low comedy for the owners of Tadich Grill. (The Eighteenth Amendment to the Constitution, decreeing

---

The Soul of the Broiler: The Charcoal

Steve Buich: "Recalling that back in Dalmatia they grilled fish over hardwood coals, my father asked Mr. Tadich if he could try it. Mr. Tadich approved of the idea and it was an instant success; that was in 1925. Prior to that, the fish was fried, baked, poached, or cooked on the griddle."

John Canepa (head chef, 1982–1996): "For the fire, we use Mexican mesquite charcoal because it has a special taste and the coals stay hot longer. Oak is also good. Madrone is by far the best, but it is so rare. If you used hardwood instead of charcoal, it would take much longer to build a good fire. Mexican charcoal is made by putting the mesquite in a pit in the ground, beginning to burn it, and then covering the pit with dirt. The wood continues to burn very slowly in the ground and turns into charcoal."

Mike Buich: "We've been getting mesquite charcoal from our supplier, Lazzari in San Francisco, for nearly 100 years. They tell me we are their oldest customer."

Prohibition, went into force January 29, 1920. It stayed in effect until the passage of the Twenty-First Amendment, repealing Prohibition, on December 5, 1933.) Louie and Tom Buich, bachelors who then shared a flat on Dolores Street, decided in 1925 to move their residence two blocks downhill to roomier accommodations. It happens that the two were the restaurant's winemakers (every decent restaurant served wine, at the least, even during Prohibition), and their cellars were situated in the basement of their flat. Quite early one Sunday, the two brothers, with the aid of friends, laid down planks and, singly and delicately, rolled ten thirty-gallon barrels of wine down the two blocks of Dolores Street. Oddly, there seemed almost to have been a police escort for the logistically difficult operation. At the end of the night, according to one account, one barrel was missing, but it turned up a week later, empty, in a vacant lot behind the police department's Mission Station a few blocks away.

These middle years of Prohibition leading to the long years of the Depression were an unpropitious time to be owners of a restaurant. But the Buich brothers held on, made modest livings, and began raising families.

■ Joseph Mertlik and Louie Buich, 1949.

World War II shook the country from its 1930s languor. It brought hundreds of thousands of people to and through San Francisco, a major port of debarkation for the Pacific theater, and it brought prosperity to the owners of the Tadich. It was a boom time for the whole town. Soldiers and sailors, about to ship out, spent their last few weeks in San Francisco. War industries like Henry Kaiser's fabled shipyards—where destroyers were built in weeks—sprang up around San Francisco. Teams of top-secret government officials set up offices in the grand old Customs House on Battery Street, two blocks from Tadich Grill's Clay Street location. Too, there were the judges, lawyers,

and police detectives from the Hall of Justice a few blocks away at Kearny between Washington and Merchant Streets. Everyone was employed, time to cook at home was scarce, and there was money to eat out at such sturdy restaurants as the Tadich.

The war brought the Tadich hundreds of new customers. These years saw the first of the famous lines of customers waiting on the sidewalk for the restaurant's doors to open for lunch. There were blackout curtains, frequent air-raid sirens, and a staff of mostly European World War I veterans.

A beef steak was always to be had at the Tadich, at least until the very end of the war, unlike the case at many other restaurants in San Francisco, especially, ironically, the steak houses. For the Tadich was known as a fish house, so the demand for beef steak among its patrons was much less. Over at the Bay City Grill, a popular steak house, steaks became so scarce that the proprietors resorted to offering chicken. Joe Mertlik had been the broiler man at the Bay City Grill for twenty-five years and found it distressingly beneath him to broil chickens instead of steaks. He asked his friends the Buiches if they needed an experienced broiler chef, and in 1943 he went to work at the Tadich, where he could broil steaks and fish. Mertlik worked at the Tadich

■ Midday staff meal in 1949. Louie Buich is the second from the left, standing.

until his retirement in 1970. A broiler chef for fifty-two years, in only two restaurants, he was, says Steve Buich, "a master of the art, in my opinion, one of the finest broiler chefs San Francisco has ever known."

Tom Buich retired in 1950, and Mitch Buich followed in 1961. Their brother Louie and his sons, Steve and Bob, then took over the ownership and operation of the restaurant. Louie suffered a major heart attack in 1952 at age fifty-five and could no longer work as chef; he died in 1965 at the age of sixty-seven. Mitch Buich was replaced as head chef by another Croatian American, Dominc Ivelich, who would serve until 1966. Ivelich had started at the restaurant in 1912, working for John Tadich. He later worked with Mitch and raised a family in San Francisco. Steve Buich remembers him as a loyal and skilled head chef with a somewhat stern, no-nonsense work ethic.

John Tadich died November 27, 1953. As one of San Francisco's newspapers put it, "San Francisco lost another link to her glamorous, cosmopolitan past yesterday with the death of John V. Tadich, pioneer restaurant operator, at the age of 98. . . . Until a few months ago, he was still having his pre-dinner martini, still rolling his own cigarettes with an imported French paper."[3]

Tadich lived to see the restaurant attain the century mark—in fact, he dined there in 1949—and a measure of the renown it now enjoys. The renown

Sole on a Sill

The Tadich's popularity sometimes spilled out onto the streets. Herb Michaels, a customer of the Tadich since the 1930s, recalls, "When the place was too crowded, it was common for Curly behind the counter to hand a plate of rex sole and a fork to a customer, who would take it over to eat on the windowsill on the Leidesdorff Street side." (Michaels also remembers the front window of F. Uri Wholesale Meats, two doors away from Tadich's, where a taxidermy stuffed two-headed calf was long displayed.)

John "Curly" Skorlich, bald as can be, was a counter waiter at the Tadich in the forties, fifties, and sixties.

■ Tom, Louie, and Mitch Buich, 1953.

began to manifest itself in the pages of food writers and San Francisco historians in the early twentieth century.

The restaurant was omitted from mention in Clarence Edwords's *Bohemian San Francisco*, published in 1914 (which described thirty-four restaurants and forty-six "Old Time Restaurants"). But the *San Francisco News Letter*, in its Diamond Jubilee edition of September 5, 1925, mentioned the restaurant prominently. And a few years after World War II, just before the restaurant turned 100, Raymond Ewell wrote of Tadich's in his 1948 *Dining Out in San Francisco,*

While I hesitate to use superlatives, I do believe that the finest seafood in San Francisco is obtainable at Tadich's. The rex sole here is unmatched, tasting like fine brook trout just out of an ice-cold mountain stream—I can't explain why Tadich's rex sole should taste better than anybody else's, but it does.[4]

Fifteen years later, in 1963, a modest San Francisco restaurant guide had this to say about the Tadich:

Strictly a men's grill with booths and counter service. Crowded at lunch with the Montgomery and California St. crowd. Some of the best seafood in town with the longtime favorite being the Rex sole.[5]

From these reviews, we know that the mid-twentieth-century favorite was rex sole. Today it is petrale sole. The Tadich now serves three times as much petrale sole as swordfish (usually caught off Southern California), king salmon (fresh from the Pacific when in season), rex sole, or sand dabs.

In that same year of 1963, Doris Muscatine, an engaging writer, historian, and food-and-wine scholar, brought out her wonderful *A Cook's Tour of San Francisco*. It provides a brief history of San Francisco restaurants generally, and short biographies of many of the city's prominent restaurants of the time. Its description of the Tadich is worth setting out substantially verbatim:

Tadich Grill . . . bustles with an energy and authority that derive from long experience, and even the size of its portions recalls days when appetites were more capacious.

For as long as any one can remember, Mr. Joseph Granat, who died recently, came every day by taxi from his jewelry store on Mission and 20th streets, to have his midday meal here. Sometimes his cab fare added up to more than his restaurant bill. One afternoon when the Giants were in town, such crowds headed for the game that no taxis were available, and he had to hire a limousine to take him back. When he couldn't make it—a rare occasion, indeed, he phoned Tadich's so that they wouldn't worry about him.

Joe Granat almost invariably sat at the counter. A few other daily counter regulars during this period were "Shy" Shenson, president of Shenson Meat Company; realtor Joe Cimino; financier Herbert Fleishhacker; Sydney Schwartz, president of Sutro Company; architect Syl Maraccini; John Figone, president

■ John "Curly" Skorlich, counter waiter from 1939 to 1966 (twenty-seven years).

■ Dominic Ivelich started working at the restaurant in 1912, and served as head chef from 1961 to 1966 (fifty-four years).

Chris Sentovich, manager from 1950 to 1957 and 1967 to 1992 (thirty-two years total). Customer Hugo Paladini is to the left, waiter John Zec to the right.

of Gold State Meat Company; Sherman Sibley, president of Pacific Gas & Electric; Ransom Cook, president of Wells Fargo Bank; Richard Ransom, successor president of Wells Fargo; and Harry East Miller, vice president of Wells Fargo.

Doris Muscatine continues with her 1963 account of the Tadich:

> The specialty of the house is fish and shellfish: broiled, baked, steamed, or fried, as well as boiled or curried. There are endless combinations of seafood that bubble together in cheese sauces, wine and mushrooms, peppers and tomatoes Creole style, or creamy smooth sauces a la Newburg. The crab sauté and deviled crab are both excellent, the crab and prawns a la Monza one of the house favorites. Sea bass and crab meat heaped on rice dressed with saffron sauce is a good dish for hearty eaters, peppery oyster and crab creole is a bit unusual, and salmon and crab cooked together a la Newburg is rich—but delicious.[6]

In 1967, redevelopment of the Clay Street area, which had once been a bustling wholesale marketplace, forced the restaurant to move after fifty-five years to its present location at 240 California Street. Dave "Garo" Sokitch had become head chef at the Tadich the year before, replacing the retiring Dominic Ivelich.

There was little advertising of the move, Sokitch recalls, but the whole city knew of it. For the last day at the Clay Street quarters, the Buiches printed a menu that reflected the 1912 prices. From his position in the kitchen, Sokitch watched the early luncheon customers that last day, a Saturday. One couple, mystified at first by the menu prices, soon whispered seditiously to each other. The man then excused himself to make a call from a pay telephone. Within thirty minutes, there were hundreds of customers waiting for a table, and television cameras were rolling.

The next day, a Sunday, the Buiches, Sokitch, and crew borrowed two trucks from Paladini's and moved the restaurant's fifty

■ Views of the interior of 545 Clay Street.

years' worth of possessions themselves. Mostly the possessions were pots and pans and papers, but there were a few oddball items, such as a 500-pound safe. A back or two was wrenched in the move.

On California Street, the Tadich's culinary tradition was carried on. Dave Sokitch continued in Dominic Ivelich's ways as head chef, just as Ivelich had continued in Mitch Buich's.

Sokitch, who had trained for two years in a culinary school in Frankfurt and had been head chef at Mayes Oyster House, added a few specials here and there but maintained the tradition of freshness in the fish and precise broiling.

Sokitch's memories of the Tadich include one in particular that unmasks the puckish humor of Bob Buich. One Friday afternoon, a man and woman arrived at the restaurant and, owing to the wait for tables, took seats at the bar. The man was eager to flaunt before his lady his knowledge of wine, and he asked for the best rosé the place had to pour. Then as now, Tadich Grill had no rosé to offer by the glass. The bartender reported the order to Bob, who contrived to accommodate the man by concocting a mixture of red and white wines that could pass for a rosé. Two glasses of this hastily made meritage were presented to the couple, and the man did the manly thing, swirling the glass, inhaling the bouquet, then savoring a sip. He exclaimed that it was the finest rosé he had tasted in his many travels, and asked what vintage it was. Bob replied, "April."

In the early 1970s, the Tadich was offering a less expensive entrée, rock cod with bay shrimps sauté, for a little over four dollars. It was an old favorite that had lost its appeal to a new generation of sophistication. Steve Buich and Sokitch sought a name change for the rock cod, and "Pacific snapper" was their answer. Sokitch recommended a significant price increase and better placement on the menu. With some reluctance, Steve Buich agreed, and the "new" dish was an instant success.

In 1949, Tadich waiter John Dukich started a guestbook, which is now filled with the signatures and comments of regulars, dignitaries, and just plain folk. After the move to California Street, the practice of keeping the guestbook was dropped for ten years, but when it resumed, the celebrities were as rife as ever. They included Jack and Marie Lord; all-star baseball players Tim McCarver and Steve Carlton; Norman Vincent Peale, who had signed the guest book twenty-two years earlier ("Back to my favorite restaurant"); Sam Jaffe ("Tadich's, our favorite"); San Francisco Fire Chief Andy Casper (Valentine's Day, 1980); David Suskind; George and Barbara Bush (making the first of several visits on September 10, 1980); Joel Grey ("Always

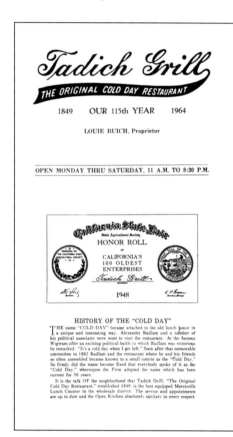

■ A typical menu cover from 1964, the restaurant's 115th year.

■ Dave Sokitch, head chef from 1966 to 1982 (sixteen years).

■ Announcement of the Tadich's move to California Street, 1967.

ANNOUNCEMENT
LAST DAY ON CLAY ST.

Tadich Grill
THE ORIGINAL COLD DAY RESTAURANT
Serving You since 1849

Due to redevelopment Tadich's will serve for the last day at 545 Clay Street on Saturday, July 15, 1967. Tadich's will be relocated at 240 California Street in order to continue serving San Francisco's Financial District in its same traditional manner.

Closing on Saturday, July 15, 1967
at 545 Clay Street
11:30 A.M.-8:30 P.M.
Bar Open 11:30 A.M.-Midnight

Opening on or about August 1, 1967 at

240 California Street
Between Front and Battery Streets
Steve and Bob Buich, Props.   SU 1-9754

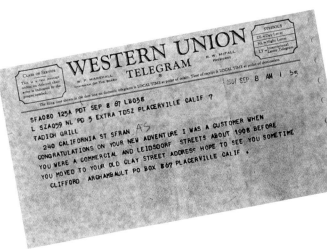

■ A telegram from a longtime customer congratulating the Buiches on their move to California Street.

■ John "Duke" Dukich, waiter from 1924 to 1966 (forty-two years).

■ Last day celebrations in the 545 Clay Street location, June 14, 1967. Steve and Bob Buich are standing left and center, respectively.

■ The demolition of the Clay Street location in 1967.

California Street

An authority on the names of San Francisco streets points out the following about California Street: "Michael Venegas, a Mexican Jesuit and author, wrote in the early 1700s, "This name [California] owed its origin to some accident; possibly to some words spoken by Indians, and misunderstood by the Spaniards." A more likely source of the name is the novel *The Adventures of Esplandian*, written by Garcia Ordonez de Montalvo and published in Toledo, Spain, in 1521. In that novel, California was the name given to a fabulous island in the Pacific, rich in minerals and precious stones and the home of a tribe of Amazons ruled by Queen Califia."[7]

All that may be. But I think the street takes its name from the state.

---

the best," December 22, 1980); Mr. and Mrs. Bill Murray ("Our honeymoon— we had to stop for food; it was good, too," February 5, 1981); Bill Christopher ("Blessings from Father Mulcahy & MASH," November 21, 1981); and Anchorage Mayor Tony Knowles (now Alaska's governor, July 28, 1982).

In 1982, after sixteen years to the day as head chef, Dave Sokitch retired, and in short order he opened his own restaurant, Garo's, on Battery Street. Located where Il Fornaio is now, Garo's failed in equally short order, and Sokitch signed on as head chef of the Cliff House. He remains fond of the Buich family and refers to his leaving the Tadich as "the biggest mistake I ever made." Sokitch was succeeded as head chef at the Tadich by award-winning chef Giacomo "John" Canepa, who had trained for three years in Lausanne, Switzerland, at the Institute Lausanne Alveccia. After his training, he had worked in France, Italy, and Canada before settling in the United States.

■ Bob and Steve Buich.

■ A view of California Street from 1858. Number 240 is the building left of center.

■ California Street in 1925.

Before Canepa took over at Tadich Grill, he was head chef at Rocca's restaurant on Golden Gate Avenue, where Stars restaurant, opened by Jeremiah Towers in 1983, is located today. Rocca's during the 1960s and 1970s was the only fine dining establishment in the Civic Center area. Lou Rocca, the owner of the restaurant, also owned Original Joe's in the Tenderloin. When Canepa, born in Genoa, took the job at Tadich Grill, Rocca asked him, "Why go with the Yugoslavians? Why not stay with the Italians?"

During Canepa's tenure, California Lieutenant Governor Leo T. McCarthy, a San Franciscan, visited Tadich's on "Tax Day," 1983. Other customers in the mid-1980s were Ralph Edwards (*This Is Your Life*); Mary Martin; Fritz Mondale; Ed Asner ("Thanks for maintaining my avoirdupois with your usually great food!"); and Elroy "Crazylegs" Hirsch, the great Los Angeles Rams flanker (1949–1957), who dined at the restaurant on January 28, 1984. Two weeks later, Gordy Soltau, tight end and place kicker for the San Francisco 49ers during virtually the same period (1950–1959), ate lunch at the Tadich. Two weeks after that, R. C. Owens, who was a flanker for the 49ers during the years its quarterbacks were Y. A. Tittle and John Brodie, took a meal there and wrote, "Wow! How wonderful." Joe Montana and Dan Marino, future Hall of Fame quarterbacks for the 49ers and Miami Dolphins, lunched there together after clashing on the turf in the 1985 game between their two teams.

A few days later, Charlton Heston stopped in for a bite to eat and commented, "Unforgettable!" CBS News's Roger Mudd dined at the Tadich on July 14, 1984, and commented, "San Francisco would die without Tadich's."

In 1989, brothers Steve and Bob Buich took Steve's son Michael as a partner in the business, installing the next generation of Buiches in the proprietorship of the business. Steve retired a few years later (maintaining a minority ownership), and when Bob retired in 2001, Mike Buich took over sole operation of the restaurant.

■ A modern view of California Street. Tadich Grill is the shorter building mid-block.

A second major quake occurred during the 140th year of the Tadich's existence. The 1989 earthquake jolted San Francisco at 5:04 P.M. on October 17, just as the third game of the World Series was about to begin at Candlestick Park between the Oakland Athletics and the San Francisco Giants.

Bob and Mike Buich had left the premises for the ballpark, and manager Chris Sentovich, who had been with the Tadich since the early 1950s, was running the place. Many proper San Franciscans were at the ballpark, but not all. Doug Haines, for one, a longtime Tadich regular, was seated at the bar, relaxing with his friend Ned Meister. A few minutes after five, Haines rolled dice with Meister for a second (his account) martini. Tipping his glass toward his buddy, Haines inexplicably lost his balance and spilled his martini onto Meister's lap. At that moment, the earthquake struck, and when one of the longest fifteen seconds in San Francisco history had passed,

■ Vice President George H. W. Bush and staff members ate at the Tadich on July 6, 1982.

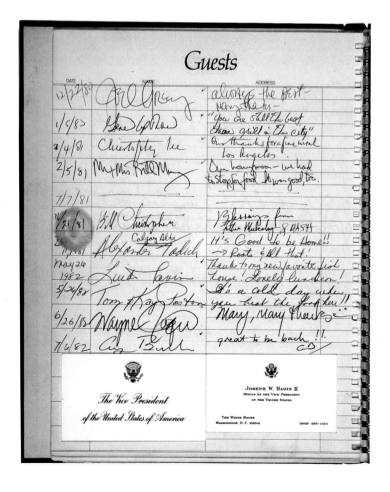

■ John Canepa, head chef from 1982 to 1996 (fourteen years).

■ A promotional picture from 1982.

Haines said to his friend, "This is the Big One, Ned." It wasn't *the* Big One, of course, but it was big.

The restaurant—like most of San Francisco—found it had no electricity or telephone service. Outside the restaurant, the blue Indian summer sky was filled with a haze of dust from the thousands of wrenched masonry buildings in downtown San Francisco. Broken glass was everywhere.

A few blocks from the Tadich, the forty-story downtown Marriott Hotel, which had celebrated its grand opening that very day, was, like other hotels in town, closing its doors. Its guests found themselves on Market Street in the warm early evening. A few of them, like many other displaced hotel guests in downtown, found their way to the Tadich.

At the Tadich, a growing crowd exhorted the bartender, "We've got ice, we've got gin, let's pour 'em!" Chris Sentovich saw the customers pouring in and decided to keep the place open. Lacking electricity, he used a hand crank to activate the ancient cash register. And Sentovich honored the crowd's exhortation in the dwindling light of the dying day, until utter darkness, save

A Day at the Tadich

5:00 A.M. On a Friday in San Francisco near the foot of California Street, the only movement at this hour is a mechanized street sweeper prowling the gutters. The only sound is the foghorn at Alcatraz. It's still dark; the cable cars on the California Street line won't run for an hour and a half yet, and six hours remain until Tadich Grill opens its doors for business.

As the street sweeper passes, Fritz Braker arrives, inserts a key, and shakes and turns the lock of the restaurant's glass- and brass-fitted wooden front doors (brought over from 545 Clay Street). Braker is the head chef of the restaurant. Going back more than seventy-five years, there have been only five other head chefs at Tadich Grill, all following a regimen that has changed little from the restaurant's earliest days.

Braker enters the restaurant and flicks switches that illuminate simple art deco chandeliers. He walks past a hundred feet of wood-paneled wall lined with brass coat hooks, on a floor of black-and-white tiles, to the kitchen. On his left runs a massive mahogany counter with a brass foot rail and twenty-eight stools. At noon a

din of diners fills this long space. At this hour, the only sound is footsteps and their echoes off the two-story-high ceiling.

Braker is joined by three others as he walks beside the bar back to the kitchen. They are his sous-chef, Adrian Dela Rosa; his broiler chef, Romy Mandap (who's been with the Tadich for twenty-seven years); and pantry chef Miguel Ortiz. A ritual nearly as old as the restaurant then begins. Braker takes inventory. Then, over glasses of hot coffee with his assistants, he makes the first notes for the day's menu. The commercial salmon season is open, and so the Pacific king salmon he'll offer—broiled, grilled, or poached—will not be farmed but wild, which most of his customers prefer. The weather has been mild, and so his suppliers should have plentiful sand dabs caught the night before.

6:00 A.M. Braker rises from his counter stool to telephone the produce and meat vendors, ordering vegetables and fruit and meats for the day, haggling over prices, alternately joking and serious. He then oversees the setting up of the kitchen.

Steel pots nearly three feet high are arrayed in a mad clangor on the eight-foot-long, inch-thick cast-iron Montague range top that dominates the front kitchen. Dela Rosa fills two pots with buckets of fresh fish stock made by the night crew. One will cook the Boston clam chowder, the other the Manhattan clam chowder. A third pot he fills with chicken stock for the soup of the day, lentil in this case. He fills another, smaller pot with cold water from a large spigot at eye level, and gives it a fistful of

salt. This pot will poach the large prawns for the day's prawn cocktails and other dishes.

Braker dices white onions, celery, and red peppers and sautés them with garlic in a dreadnought skillet for the mixture that will make the crab cakes. The skillet is so large, Braker has to hold it with both hands to toss the sautéing vegetables.

A distinctive and almost cultishly popular tartar sauce is one of the secrets of Tadich Grill. Ortiz becomes bashful when I find my way into the early-morning kitchen and watch him at work with a massive ricer making the sauce. He's at it the better part of an hour.

7:00 A.M. Braker telephones the first of the Tadich's three seafood vendors, the California Shellfish Company. He calls the LaRocca and Friscia companies next. The chef's mission is every day the same—to get the best and the freshest fish and shellfish at the best price to be had. He'll almost always order ninety pounds of petrale sole and thirty pounds each of swordfish, salmon, clams, shrimp, and cleaned crabmeat. When they are available he'll also order shad roe (usually only in June), escolar, Chilean sea bass, rock cod (now usually called Pacific snapper), ahi or yellowjack tuna, and monkfish. For the customer for whom price is no object, or perhaps for whom a great price is an object, the chef will order lobster and abalone. This day escolar and monkfish are both available, and he orders twenty pounds apiece. The fishing fleet hauled in both sand

dabs and rex sole, and Braker orders thirty pounds apiece of them as well.

7:30 A.M. Owner Mike Buich arrives and meets with his head chef. They confer over the menu, and Buich hands it over to the printer. Each day's menu is printed anew.

10:30 A.M. Mandap slides the grate from the broiler top, piles pieces of mesquite charcoal in a mound, and lights the fire. Thirty minutes later the coals are gray.

11:00 A.M. A crowd of as many as fifty has been waiting for an early lunch. Mike Buich unlocks the doors, admits and seats them, and gives them menus, and waiters begin to shout orders to the kitchen. Within a half hour the place is full, the din is electric, and the wait for tables begins and grows.

for the emergency exit lights, made the pouring of even the most elemental of drinks impossible.

At Candlestick Park, the Giants and A's decided they'd play game three of their World Series another day. After darkness forced the Tadich to lock up, Haines ended up in a friend's Pacific Heights apartment. To the south, he could see the generator-lit lamps of San Francisco General Hospital, and to the north the fires raging in the Marina District that destroyed much of that lovely neighborhood. All else was dark.

The 1906 earthquake had put The Cold Day Restaurant—and virtually all of the rest of San Francisco—out of commission for months or years. The 1989 quake, however, did no damage to the building at 240 California Street (built in 1908) where Tadich Grill is housed. The restaurant was closed for only the evening of the earthquake and the day immediately following. The next morning, Thursday, October 19, Mike Buich and chef John Canepa arrived at the restaurant early and discovered that they had power but no gas. They quickly developed a mini-menu composed of crab louis, deep-fried prawns, and char-broiled fish. A surprising number of well-wishers came by the restaurant to confirm that it had survived the quake; they were served complimentary Bloody Marys by a thankful Mike Buich. In all, the restaurant served about 250 lunches that day. That night, gas was restored and the Tadich was open for regular business by Friday, October 20. The Bay Bridge lay fractured for months; the Marina District was rubble a lot longer; but Tadich Grill on this occasion scarcely missed a beat.

Tadich's Daily Specials

Fritz Braker (current head chef): "Tadich features about ten different specials every day, but some are traditional on certain days of the week. On Mondays, we have a boiled brisket of beef. On Tuesdays, it's beef tongue and pot roast. Wednesdays we do a roasted chicken. Corned beef and cabbage are always on Thursdays. And Fridays we have a baked shoulder of lamb. Once a month I make a nice old-fashioned Irish stew. If we have any leftovers, of course, we have to feed about twenty employees every day. So that takes care of that."

San Francisco Sourdough

In his published reminiscences of San Francisco and the mother lode country from 1849 to 1857, Howard Gardiner recalled the miners baking bread. The ingredients mixed, the miner had to knead the dough, set it aside until it had risen to twice its size, and then bake it in a covered pot buried in a bed of coals. The miner reserved a dollop of dough from each batch as the starter for his next loaf. Wary of thieves, he took the starter, and pot, with him to bed. The starter gave the bread, for whatever reason, a distinctive sour taste. That was the beginning of San Francisco sourdough bread.[8]

Fritz Braker: "We buy all our bread from Parisian, which has been in San Francisco since 1856. The bread is an issue at Tadich Grill. We go through about 140 two-pound loaves a day. Seventy at lunch and seventy at dinner. Beautiful sourdough bread. And we are very particular. We're the only restaurant they bake specially for in the old way, the way the Buiches want it. The bread is very established and our customers, especially the old-timers, know exactly how it has to be. It's nice and crusty outside and beautifully lightly sour inside. It's another one of these things, you know; it's a tradition."

■ Partners Bob, Steve, and Mike Buich, 1993.

In 1996, Swiss-born Fritz Braker became only the sixth head chef at
Tadich Grill in seventy-five years, succeeding John Canepa. After training in
Switzerland at the same school John Canepa attended, Braker worked many
kitchens, in Europe, Canada, and the United States. He had been the execu-
tive chef at the Grand Hyatt in San Francisco, overseen food preparation in
five dining rooms at the Hyatt Regency in Waikiki, and in between had
owned and cooked at his own place, a small Swiss restaurant in Vancouver,
British Columbia. When Canepa announced his retirement, one of the Tadich's
fish purveyors introduced Braker to the Buiches. Braker and Canepa cooked
together for two weeks to ensure, as Mike said, that "our customers didn't
notice the change in chefs." Braker, like Canepa before him, and Sokitch and
Ivelich and Mitch and Louie Buich before them, has carried on the Tadich's
cooking tradition, with only the subtlest of changes.

In 1998, as the restaurant approached an extraordinary milestone, its 150th anniversary, the James Beard Foundation of New York gave the Tadich its award for being an "American Regional Classic."

The year 1999 marked that milestone—the 150th anniversary, the virtually unpronounceable sesquicentennial, of the restaurant's founding. Only a handful of restaurants in the world are older (and, one could argue, none of them is superior). London, for example, is nearly two thousand years older than San Francisco, yet its oldest restaurant is but fifty-one years longer in the tooth than the Tadich.

The Tadich to some may not be the greatest restaurant in the United States, but to very many it's the greatest oldest.

Round-Nosed Sole Overthrows Rex

"Round-nosed sole," as former mayor Joseph L. Alioto recalled petrale sole being called, has overthrown rex sole as the true "king" of sole. The Tadich now buys about ninety pounds of petrale sole a day—"pure poundage" in Bob Buich's words, or filleted. By contrast, the restaurant buys only about thirty pounds apiece of whole rex sole and sand dabs, which, of course, must be pan-dressed and deboned for customers. So, as current head chef Fritz Baker puts it, "we probably have three or four orders of petrale for every order of rex."

Not Only No Reservations

It wasn't until 1989, the year of the "little earthquake," that the restaurant started taking credit cards. Until then it was cash only, with an occasional hand-maintained account. It still doesn't take reservations. And there are no tables for one.

Chapter 6

THE CITY:
Peacetime to Culinary Modernity

"In the window I smelled all the food of San Francisco."

—JACK KEROUAC

While the quality of the city's cuisine did not decline in the postwar years, little exciting was happening, at least to the gastronome. The end of World War II left the people of San Francisco, like all Americans, enervated. It was an era of ennui and restiveness in the country. Americans were weary of the two wars, and of the intervening Prohibition and Depression, and they wanted, if only briefly, to forget the new angry armies of foreign menaces, some of whom had only recently been allies. Americans sought just to get back to work, marry, raise families, and cultivate new middle-class values.

At least that's what a lot of Americans thought, until Jack Kerouac captured the soul of the next lost American generation in *On the Road*, published in 1955. Kerouac made many Americans rethink what they thought were their values. Sometimes he did it hungry. At the end of chapter 10, in early 1950s San Francisco, a forlorn Sal Paradise (a thinly disguised Kerouac) decides in a wry way not to die; he takes in the food smells of the city:

In the window I smelled all the food of San Francisco. There were seafood places out there where the buns were hot, and the baskets were good enough to eat too; where the menus themselves were soft with foody esculence as though dipped in hot broths and roasted dry and good enough to eat too. Just show me the bluefish spangle on a seafood menu and I'd eat it; let me smell the drawn butter and lobster claws. There were places where they specialized in thick red roast beef *au jus,* or roast chicken basted in wine. There were places where hamburgs sizzled on grills and the coffee was only a nickel. And oh, that pan-fried chow mein flavored air that blew into my room from Chinatown, vying with the spaghetti sauces of North Beach, the soft-shell crab of Fisherman's Wharf—nay, the ribs of Fillmore turning on spits! Throw in the Market Street chili beans, redhot, and french-fried potatoes of the Embarcadero wino night, and steamed clams from Sausalito across the bay, and that's my ah-dream of San Francisco. Add fog, hunger-making raw fog, and the throb of neons in the soft night, the clack of high-heeled beauties, white doves in a Chinese grocery window.[1]

Kerouac never lived well enough in San Francisco to taste and describe its better cuisine. In this passage, he exhales the essence of common food in San Francisco as it was inhaled in the streets and from lifted window sashes in the postwar years, and as it still is.

The Oldest Restaurant in the United States?

The oldest restaurant in the United States is generally thought to be Boston's Union Oyster House, founded in 1826. It is presumably Boston's oldest restaurant as well.

New York's senior eatery may be the Fraunces Tavern Restaurant, at 54 Pearl Street in Manhattan. But since the Fraunces Tavern was founded in 1769, a question arises regarding how the Union Oyster House, established fifty-seven years later, can claim to be the *country's* oldest restaurant. It was in the Fraunces Tavern, now owned by the Sons of the Revolution, that George Washington bade farewell to his officers on December 4, 1783.

When told of the Union Oyster House's claim to be the country's oldest restaurant, a manager at the Fraunces Tavern shrugged and said, "If Boston needs that distinction, that's fine—they can have it. But by the way, our tea party was better than theirs."

After the Fraunces Tavern, New York's oldest restaurants are Gage and Tollner (founded 1879) and Peter Luger Steak House (1887), both in Brooklyn.

Many of the oldest San Francisco restaurants thrived as the century moved into the Kennedy years, the 1960s and beyond. Besides the Tadich, two in particular were the Old Clam House and Jack's.

The Old Clam House was the scene of a wake after the sad seventh game of the 1962 World Series, played at Candlestick Park, which was lost when Willie McCovey's ninth-inning, two-out line drive was snared by Yankees second baseman Bobby Richardson to end the Giants's chances at a championship. As he had many times before, Herb Caen wrote about the Old Clam House and McCovey's "shot" a few months before he died:

> Getting back to Old S.F. and where did it go, the Old Clam House on Bayshore turns 135 this weekend. Great memories there of the '62 World Series, with the whole place sobbing drunkenly into the dawn over McCovey's line drive that magically gets higher by the year. Actually, your Little League brother could've caught it.[2]

"Saturday lunch at Jack's," Caen wrote in 1961, was one of life's great pleasures, "where (the weekday pressure off) it's perfectly okay to dawdle for three hours over your second bottle of Chateau Magdeleine."[3] Louis Lurie, the San Francisco real estate tycoon (they were called that then), lunched at Jack's almost daily from 1916 until his death at the age of eighty-four in 1972. His was the round table beneath the staircase leading to the second floor. Following Lurie's death, Caen wrote,

> Whenever you walked into Jack's, you peeked to the right to see who Lurie had as guests that day—Gertrude Lawrence or Noel Coward, Somerset Maugham or Arthur Godfrey, Maurice Chevalier or Sammy Davis. Sometimes it was only politicians or newspaper bums, as he called us.[4]

In 1968, Caen lunched at Jack's with Senator Robert F. Kennedy and wrote a surpassingly good column about the occasion. Five months after that lunch, Kennedy, then the front-runner in the race for the Democratic presidential nomination, was assassinated in Los Angeles the night of the California primary election.

Caen broke the story of the sale and temporary closure of Jack's in the opening item of his column of December 12, 1996, one of the last he wrote:

> SCOOPLETTE: Jack's, the city's most venerable restaurant—same address (615 Sacramento) since 1864, same waiters (wellll, almost), same tablecloths—has just been sold by Jack Redinger to young John Konstin, who owns John's Grill on Ellis, no spring chicken itself. Konstin, who says he paid $1.32 million for the three-story landmark, will close it December 31 for a million bucks worth of retrofitting and gussying up to ensure that Jack's will survive. Let us hope that the town's most beloved group of curmudgeonly waiters does likewise.[5]

When the old Jack's closed New Year's Eve, 1996, the place was packed, above and below decks, with revelers celebrating not so much New Year's Eve as the passing of an era. When it shut its doors that night, there was not a scrap of spinach or a spare fillet of sole, much less a bottle of Jordan Cabernet left behind. When Redinger telephoned Dominique Thollot, the longtime headwaiter (and real manager of Jack's) early on New Year's morning, he said only, "Turn off the gas in the kitchen." No sentimental good-byes from the old owner.

Dominique announced his retirement from Jack's, where he had waited on tables for nearly forty years, a few months before Redinger told Herb Caen he was selling the restaurant. Even before the announcement of the

San Francisco's Favorite Waiter

There are a thousand stories of Dominique Thollot. I'll spare you mine, but will share this one, from Herb Caen's column of March 24, 1995:

> Paul Bancroft, the prominent San Franciscan who died Mon. at 90, and his wife, Kitty, who died in 1981, had a William Powell–Myrna Loy kind of marriage. Every Sunday night, they dined at Jack's, starting with martinis and ending with cognacs, but after Kitty died, Paul stayed away from Jack's for years. When he finally returned, beloved waiter Dominique brought him cognac after dinner. "I didn't order that," said Paul, at which Dominique pointed his finger heavenward and whispered, "She did."[6]

sale, San Francisco had decided to put on a party for Dominique, whom Caen had described so often as "San Francisco's favorite waiter." The party was held January 16, 1997, in Palio d'Asti, a superb northern Italian restaurant across the street from the dark Jack's. It seemed that all of San Francisco's power and society turned out for the occasion. In the middle of the speech-making, an Englishman paying homage to Dominique asked, "What other city in the world would pay such a tribute to a waiter?"

Jack's reopened in the fall of 1998, about a year and a half after it closed, and with a stunning skylight to boot. Especially given the legal and code restrictions Konstin had to comply with, he did a magnificent job. But he sold the place so that it could be made into offices at the end of 2000, and it seemed that Jack's had at last met its demise. However, the market for office space cratered in 2001, and San Franciscans were heartened to learn that Napa chef Philippe Jeanty bought the building and opened a new restaurant there in 2002 called Jeanty at Jack's, "Est. 1864."

Near the end of the 1960s, or the beginning of the 1970s—just when is hard to tell—a food renaissance began in the San Francisco Bay Area. It may have begun with the opening in 1971 of an unprepossessing little restaurant on Shattuck Avenue in Berkeley: Chez Panisse, owned and operated by Alice Waters. It remains one of the best restaurants in the Bay Area. What distinguished Alice Waters's restaurant was a new simplicity and an insistence on freshness exemplified by the vegetable garden in back of the restaurant. The vegetables served in the restaurant were picked that day.

Waters was inspired by the French writer Curnonsky (Maurice Edmond Sailland, 1872–1956). Curnonsky stressed the importance of ingredients over preparation, writing, "Make it simple, let things taste of what they are." Waters was puzzled for some time by the simplicity of many of his recipes but then came to realize that the key was the quality and freshness of the ingredients.[7]

Some of the best chefs in the country have trained at Chez Panisse and have gone on to become stars in their own right. Among them are Paul Bertolli (Oliveto, Oakland), Deborah Madison (Greens at Fort Mason in San Francisco), Mark Peel (Spago, Los Angeles), Jonathan Waxman, Mark Miller (formerly of the Fourth Street Grill, Berkeley), Judy Rodgers (Union Hotel in

Benicia, Zuni Cafe in San Francisco), and on and on. One of the best-known protégés of Waters is Jeremiah Tower, formerly of Stars in San Francisco.

The new cuisine, in San Francisco and throughout the country, is too vast a subject for this chapter, or this book. But a few words should be said about Masa's, one of the best of the new bunch, in the view of many. Masa's opened in the Vintage Court Hotel in 1983, under the guidance of head chef Masa Kobayashi, who had previously been head chef at Auberge du Soleil in the Napa Valley. When it opened, the restaurant was immediately acclaimed as perhaps the best in the country, or the world. A little over a year after opening his restaurant, Masa was murdered brutally in the vestibule of his home in a case that is still unsolved.

Then, "something of a miracle took place. Sous-chef Bill Galloway stepped into Kobayashi's shoes and performed flawlessly. And rather than simply imitating what Kobayashi did, Galloway slowly introduced new dishes, lightened the sauces, *and made the food better than it ever had been.*" (Italics added.) So wrote the *San Francisco Chronicle*'s restaurant critic on April 3, 1987, just as Julian Serrano was about to take over from Galloway and assume the mantle of Masa's head chef. The reviewer went on, "Masa's is my nominee for the best French restaurant in the United States, an accolade more generally accorded Lutece in New York." Ron Siegel is now the head chef, and the restaurant still receives rave reviews.

Despite the demise of many of the grand old places, the restaurant trade in San Francisco is flourishing. No one knows the exact number, but there are today between 2,500 and 3,000 restaurants in San Francisco. That works out to about one restaurant for every 250 to 300 citizens.[8] This is little short of remarkable, considering that there are some San Franciscans (infants, the infirm) who don't eat out often.

Indeed, the restaurant trade is more than flourishing. Despite the closures, San Francisco and the Bay Area are still considered a center of the culinary arts—even in New York. The prestigious James Beard Foundation of New York annually presents what have come to be known as the "Oscars of the food industry." In 1996, it named Jeremiah Tower of San Francisco's Stars restaurant the country's outstanding chef. In 1997, the award went to Thomas Keller, the chef-owner of the French Laundry in Yountville in the Napa Valley, just north of San Francisco. In the same year, the Beard Foundation named Michael Mina, the chef at San Francisco's Aqua, the nation's "rising star chef of the year." Rose Pistola, Reed Hearon's Italian restaurant in San Francisco's North Beach, was named the country's best new restaurant. Alice Waters was given the humanitarian of the year award. The regional chef-of-the-year award for California went to Hubert Keller, owner and chef at San Francisco's Fleur de Lys. The only major Beard Foundation award not taken by San Francisco in 1997 was that for the country's outstanding restaurant. The Beard Foundation

■ Among its numerous awards, the Tadich received an honor award from the city of San Francisco in 1967.

■ Lintel above the Tadich's door on California Street.

gave that award to one of its city's own, Danny Meyer's Union Square Cafe in New York. Masa's restaurant of San Francisco was one of the five nominees for that award.[9] In succeeding years, San Francisco restaurants have continued to fare well, earning awards from the Beard Foundation and other organizations.

In one sense, perhaps, culinary trends have simply caught up with Tadich Grill. The seafood it serves must be the freshest available, and so must the vegetables and produce. In another sense, the recently opened restaurants have broken new ground. Their dishes feature unexpected combinations and adorn themselves elaborately in whorls and towers of colorful presentation. Their portions, though, sometimes seem better suited to the dieter than to the traditional San Francisco diner. No one has been known to have departed the Tadich complaining of hunger.

Chapter 7

THE RESTAURANT:
Celebrity Reminiscences and Miscellaneous Zaniness

"San Francisco without Tadich's would not be San Francisco."

—HERB CAEN

Like San Francisco's John's Grill, which is mentioned in Dashiell Hammett's *The Maltese Falcon*, published in 1928, Tadich's has made the literary scene in a way. On April 19, 1995, Patrick O'Brian, the great Irish writer of novels of the Napoleonic sea wars, and the limner of the characters Aubrey and Maturin, appeared at the Herbst Theater in San Francisco, where he was interviewed by American poet laureate Robert Hass. Recounting his reading of *War and Peace*, O'Brian asked, "Can I put in a parenthesis about pudding? I'm very attached to pudding. I've just reached the point very early in *War and Peace* where Natasha calls out, 'Mama, what's for pudding?' When I was a child I very frequently asked, 'What's for pudding?' I can't tell you the attachment for pudding of the Irish, and the English for that matter. I live in France, and the French haven't a notion of pudding. And this sounds deeply ungrateful, but I haven't found a great quality of puddings in the States."

Hass then turned to the audience and asked, "Can anyone recommend a pudding in San Francisco?" From the audience a woman's voice answered, "Bread pudding at Tadich's." To which Hass echoed, "Ah yes, the bread pudding at Tadich's." O'Brian responded, "I shall have to try that. I suffered bread pudding as a child."

A postscript should be appended in the interest of veracity. Tadich's has forever served a rice custard pudding, but never a bread pudding.

In the 1980s, Patricia Unterman, owner of the Hayes Street Grill and restaurant critic for the *San Francisco Chronicle*, wrote this brief review of the Tadich:

> The ancient dark wood paneling, the booths that enclose white-linen-covered tables, bentwood chairs, the cracked plaster ceilings, and the veteran waiters all give Tadich its splendid ambience . . . . Ask your waiter what's fresh that day, and if it's the generously cut salmon or swordfish order it rare if you want it moist in the middle. Tadich is justly famous for its buttery grilled sand dabs, rex sole and petrale sole, all local fish. The fancier preparations don't hold up to today's standards, but the rice custard pudding and baked apples certainly do.[1]

A survey of menus from the Tadich shows a remarkable consistency in offerings and, hence, in the tastes of San Franciscans. I have found a special menu from the day The Original Cold Day Restaurant reopened in 1912, after the breakup of the Tadich-Sutich joint venture. It is short on variety, but it and later menus reflect the longevity of the Tadich.

The opening-day menu for August 26, 1912, offered as its salad course a Crab Tadich Special, and for soup a Chicken Consommé au Vermicelli. Fried sand dabs à la meunière, sweetbread patties "financier," ravioli and cheese Napolitaine, and spring chicken with garden peas were the entrées. For dessert, the offerings were ice cream, cakes, cheese and fruits, and café noir. That was it.

By 1916, the menu had expanded considerably. A cracked crab (in season) was thirty-five cents, as was a "plain steak." A T-bone was sixty-five cents, a porterhouse ten cents more. There was "fish to order," depending on what was available and fresh from the markets across the street. A quart of the house's best "cabernet claret" wine, from CALWA (the cooperative California Wine

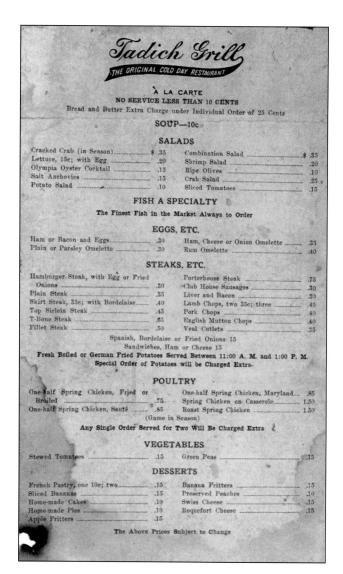

Tadich Grill

THE ORIGINAL COLD DAY RESTAURANT

À LA CARTE

NO SERVICE LESS THAN 10 CENTS

Bread and Butter Extra Charge under Individual Order of 25 Cents

SOUP—10c

SALADS

Cracked Crab (in Season)	$ .35	Combination Salad	$ .35
Lettuce, 15c; with Egg	.20	Shrimp Salad	.20
Olympia Oyster Cocktail	.15	Ripe Olives	.10
Salt Anchovies	.15	Crab Salad	.25
Potato Salad	.10	Sliced Tomatoes	.15

FISH A SPECIALTY

The Finest Fish in the Market Always to Order

EGGS, ETC.

Ham or Bacon and Eggs	.30	Ham, Cheese or Onion Omelette	.35
Plain or Parsley Omelette	.30	Rum Omelette	.40

STEAKS, ETC.

Hamburger Steak, with Egg or Fried Onions	.30	Porterhouse Steak	.75
		Club House Sausages	.20
Plain Steak	.35	Liver and Bacon	.30
Skirt Steak, 35c; with Bordelaise	.40	Lamb Chops, two 35c; three	.45
Top Sirloin Steak	.45	Pork Chops	.40
T-Bone Steak	.65	English Mutton Chops	.40
Fillet Steak	.50	Veal Cutlets	.35

Spanish, Bordelaise or Fried Onions 15

Sandwiches, Ham or Cheese 15

Fresh Boiled or German Fried Potatoes Served Between 11:00 A. M. and 1:00 P. M.

Special Order of Potatoes will be Charged Extra

POULTRY

One-half Spring Chicken, Fried or Broiled	.75	One-half Spring Chicken, Maryland	.85
		Spring Chicken en Casserole	1.50
One-half Spring Chicken, Sauté	.85	Roast Spring Chicken	1.50

(Game in Season)

Any Single Order Served for Two Will Be Charged Extra

VEGETABLES

Stewed Tomatoes	.15	Green Peas	.15

DESSERTS

French Pastry, one 10c; two	.15	Banana Fritters	.15
Sliced Bananas	.15	Preserved Peaches	.10
Home-made Cakes	.10	Swiss Cheese	.15
Home-made Pies	.10	Roquefort Cheese	.15
Apple Fritters	.15		

The Above Prices Subject to Change

■ A menu from 1916.

Association) was a dollar, as was a quart of Vine Clif Riesling. No chardonnay or sauvignon blanc was offered. Napa soda water was ten cents, Vichy water three times that price.

With the outbreak of World War II, the price structure changed noticeably. A *half* cracked crab was sixty cents in June of 1942. A T-bone steak was $1.50 in June, but would be $2 in November. Likewise, the porterhouse that went for $1.75 in June sold for $2.25 in November. Fresh fish, though, remained abundant on the menu and constant in price. Fish was too perishable to ship to the troops overseas, and so it stayed stateside for the folks at home.

House white wine was sixty cents a bottle in June 1942, and the house red was fifty cents. In November of that year, the restaurant was offering Beaulieu Vineyards chablis or Burgundy for $1.25 a bottle.

By war's end, the toll on the nation's beef supply was apparent from the menu at the Tadich. A menu from August 18, 1945, four days after V-J Day, offered no T-bone or porterhouse (although a "tenderloin steak" is listed, at $1.50). Cracked crab was offered, though, and had miraculously dropped in price to eighty-five cents. Other seafood remained a staple, and at relatively stable prices. Beaulieu Vineyard wines had crept up to $1.50 a bottle, but Vichy water, whether out of loyalty to the Free French or simple unavailability, was no longer offered.

In the 1950s, the menu changed little, though prices eased upward with the inflation of the postwar years. In 1951, broiled pompano—a rare delicacy in San Francisco even today—made its appearance on the menu, at $1.65.

A New York steak was $3.25, and Beaulieu Vineyard wines went for two dollars a bottle. In 1954, petrale first appeared on the menu; it was not even referred to as sole, round-nosed or otherwise.

The help at Tadich Grill (like the owners) has been heavily weighted with men of Croatian descent. And many have been fluent in Slavic, a fact that has, on occasion, caused havoc.

In the 1960s, John Markovich, the Tadich's resident practical joker, made the short stature of his fellow waiter Chris Zarich the subject of endless abuse. One afternoon, a family of four quite short people came to the restaurant for a meal. Scarcely containing himself, Markovich giggled in Slavic to Zarich,

---

Dukich, Skorlich, and Markovich, aka Duke, Curly, and Frenchy

There's no denying that great waiters help make great restaurants. Three of the Tadich's great waiters were named "John," though no one knew them by that name.

In a restaurant with a knack for longevity, John "Duke" Dukich had his. He worked at Tadich Grill for forty-two years, from 1924 until 1966. With no formal education beyond the mandatory six grades of elementary school in Croatia, he displayed a phenomenal command of mathematics. He could play four games of liars' dice at once, never once taking a second look at the dice beneath his box, and all the while serving his customers. They knew him only as "Duke."

John Skorlich, also a native of Croatia, jumped ship in the Far East as a teenaged ship's mate. He made it to San Francisco and began working at the Tadich in 1939. From then until he retired from the restaurant in 1966 (a reign of twenty-seven years), he was known as "Curly." He was, naturally enough, bald as a proverbial billiard ball.

The third John was John Markovich, who worked at the Tadich for twenty-seven years, from 1943 until 1970. Also a native of Croatia, Markovich worked the front station, closest to the door, where his smile and humor were handy. Markovich's nickname—to his fellow workers and his customers—was "Frenchy," for he was ever ready with the French line or phrase or bon mot. On account of his fluency, Steve Buich once seated a group of French tourists at Markovich's table. Flush-faced, and found out, Markovich confessed to Steve that he knew only a few words of French, and could hardly converse in the language. He gave the French folks good service notwithstanding.

"Your relatives are here." Steve Buich, having watched and heard the whole scene, then sat the family at a table where Markovich, still convulsed in laughter, would be their waiter.

On another occasion, waiter Mario Ivanov, helping a woman off with her topcoat, praised in fulsome Slavic the beauty of a particular prominence of her body. Smiling, she turned to Ivanov and replied, *"Hvala"*— "Thank you" in Slavic.

Once a young Croatian waiter (not knowing who his customer was) served State Senator George N. Zenovich of Fresno a plate of oysters. As he did he muttered in Slavic, "Eat all you want, old man; they won't help you." The senator, without so much as an upward glance, rejoined in impeccable Slavic, "You no doubt need them more than I do."

■ Waiter John "Frenchy" Markovich worked at the Tadich from 1943 to 1970 (twenty-seven years).

■ Old-timers reunion luncheon, 1998. Standing, left to right: Marty Rado, bartender for eight years; Nick Cupich, waiter for eleven years; Dave Sokitch, chef for sixteen years; Mike Buich; Steve Buich; John Scopazzi, waiter for fourteen years; Mario Ivanov, waiter for twenty-nine years; Bob Buich; Joe Scopazzi, waiter for twenty-two years. Seated, left to right: John Canepa, chef for fourteen years; Ivo Semolic, waiter for thirty-two years; Donna Umeki, accountant for fourteen years.

Several years ago, I asked Steve Buich to recount his more colorful and memorable customers. He recalled a gentleman who had been a customer of the Tadich for at least fifty years. Once a year, this customer would call to arrange for a private party of twenty or so, to be held at ten o'clock on a Saturday night (when the restaurant was officially closed).

"Usually it was a wild duck feed, and the customer would supply the ducks himself early the morning of the party," Steve said. "Promptly at ten o'clock on the appointed evening, the regular customers having left, the gentleman would arrive with his group; then the party began!" There would be appetizers and cocktails, stories and song. Then, just after two o'clock in the morning, after the many courses of the meal and many glasses of wine, the man would rouse himself from conversation, thank his guests, and show them the door. He would then make out a check to Tadich Grill, leave the amount blank, sign it, and ask Steve Buich to fill it in for whatever he thought "was right." More than mildly curious, I asked who the fellow was. Steve replied, "Some great old trial lawyer from the Valley. Anthony Chargin." I smiled at the coincidental ways of the world. Tony Chargin had been my long-deceased father's partner and is my godfather.

***

Anthony J. Chargin: Sportsman and Bon Vivant

Steve Buich: "Tony Chargin was very easy to get to know when I first started working at Tadich Grill. He was very large, very outgoing, spoke the same language as we did, and was very much the sportsman. And there was always a song—what a beautiful voice he had! Many times he would come in with numerous friends from Stockton and they would stay at the Fairmont Hotel. They would come down to the restaurant for their after-hours party, and we would have their ducks all seasoned and ready to go. We would keep two cooks and two waiters and they would stay there until one or two o'clock in the morning.

"Well now, Monday morning, when I was going over the receipts for the weekend, I would come upon this blank check and I would carefully take up the receipt for his party, with all of the charges. And so I would tally up so many duck dinners, so many bottles of wine, so many salads, and so forth, and itemize the bill and send him a carefully documented receipt. The next time he came in he would scold me for having gone through the effort of doing that and tell me to simply write the amount in on his check in the future."

■ A matchbook from
the Clay Street days.

In the spring of 1997, shortly before his death, Joe Alioto, the brilliant and flamboyant mayor of San Francisco from 1968 until 1976, reminisced over sand dabs and white wine at Tadich Grill:

> I knew Tadich when it was located on Clay Street. When I was about twelve years old, I used to work in my father's wholesale fish market. Tadich was in the center of the three leading wholesale fish markets in town at that time. They were Paladini's; my dad's company, the San Francisco International Fish Company (the "International" because we used to ship a lot of salmon to Germany in those days); and Western California Fish Company, which was run by my mother's cousins, the Caitos. Tadich was literally right in the middle. In those days, the boats used to come in the night before. The market was open at four o'clock in the morning, and all of the sand dabs and the rex sole and the round-nosed sole—we didn't use the word "petrale" in those days—would come in. So the fish that was filleted at five o'clock in the morning would be served at Tadich for lunch or dinner.
>
> Because of that association, we used to eat lunch at Tadich a good deal. And on festive occasions, our dad would bring us down to Tadich or the Manger, which was up near the city prison at that point, the present site of the United Nations Chinese Hotel. So those are my early recollections of Tadich.
>
> As I grew older, I became attached to what we used to call the San Francisco sawdust restaurants.[2]

It was a common practice in those bustling places to spread sawdust on the floors, even in the dining rooms, to soak up spillage and reduce slippage. The premises were swept after lunchtime, and fresh sawdust was spread for the evening period.

> They included Sam's Grill; Jack's; Big Ben's Grill, which was up here on Montgomery Street; Tadich; and the Old Grotto Restaurant, which literally was next door to my dad's wholesale fish place. Big Ben's Grill went the way of all flesh, the Old Grotto went the way of all flesh, and the Manger went the way of all flesh. But Jack's remains, Sam's remains, and the Tadich remains.

Jack's, as I mentioned earlier, closed in 2001 but revived in 2002.

As it happens, Mr. Alioto's association with his father's fish company indirectly—or perhaps not so indirectly—led to his career as a great trial lawyer:

I worked at my father's fish company, so would go in with him early in the morning. I worked in a little order office, where men used to—let's say they were doing something for Tadich or Jack's—they'd make up the order and call it out, and I'd write it down—twenty-five pounds of halibut, twelve pounds of sand dabs. . . .

I worked there in the summertime. But I used to spend a lot of time in the criminal courts, which were a block up the way. They had great lawyers like Garret McEnerney, and as a young kid I used to go watch them.

I was compelled to ask, "Was it that experience that prompted you not to enter the fish business, but to become a lawyer instead?" His Honor's unequivocal answer was, "Yes."

Tastes change, even in San Francisco's North Beach, the traditional neighborhood of San Francisco's Italian community, and its fishermen. Mayor Alioto recalled,

■ Joseph L. Alioto, mayor of San Francisco from 1968 to 1976.

At home, we used to eat what we then thought of as peasant fish—shrimp, and crab, oysters, and caviar from Sacramento River sturgeon. There was a crazy law. It was illegal to be caught in possession of a sturgeon, but not illegal to be caught in possession of the caviar. So the fishermen used to give my dad the caviar, which was never sold.

"Who got to eat the great steaks from the sturgeon?" I asked.

"They were bootlegged in some way; I don't know how," he replied. Mayor Alioto continued,

The current redwood grove at the TransAmerica building, the minipark, is the site of my father's old fish company. Across Clay Street from where Tadich was. So deliveries were very easy. There were no delivery costs involved with Tadich between Paladini, where he mainly bought, and my dad, when he had certain species of fish that Paladini might not have had. Or Western Cal too. Paladini and my father each had their own boat. Of course they bought crabs and fish from the fishermen as well, but they had their own boats. The thing about Tadich is you get seafood treats you don't find anywhere else. Such a variety of things. The sautéed crab legs, the clams—I love steamed clams. The one thing they don't make here that I've been trying to get them to make is oregano clams, baked clams oregano, with fresh oregano. That they don't do.

At this point, the waiter asked whether Mr. Alioto would like broccoli, and he replied no, but he would like string beans, sautéed. Asked whether he would like them sautéed with garlic he replied "No, I don't like garlic." *That* from an Italian mayor of San Francisco, born and raised in North Beach.

Joe Alioto was by no means the only San Francisco mayor to have had a particular fondness for Tadich Grill. Elmer Robinson, mayor from 1948 to 1956, was a regular, as was George Christopher, who served from 1956 until 1964. A frequent customer at the Tadich, Christopher wrote in the restaurant's guestbook on May 15, 1985, "The greatest!" Christopher, who promoted the Bay Area's rapid-transit system, conceived of the Golden Gateway Center, and seduced the New York Giants to move to San Francisco, died September 14, 2000, at the age of ninety-two, a Tadich regular to the end.

Frank Jordan, former police chief and mayor of San Francisco from 1992 to 1996, also frequented Tadich's. When he dined at the restaurant on March 25, 1992, shortly after taking office, he too scrawled superlatives in the guestbook.

Willie L. Brown, Jr., who held the speakership of the California Assembly longer than any other person in the state's history, defeated Jordan in a dramatic race for mayor of San Francisco in 1995, and took office the following January. He may be the most colorful and charismatic mayor of San Francisco—not to mention the most politically astute—since Sunny Jim Rolph, who served as mayor for nearly twenty years, from 1912 until 1931. If so, in these respects he eclipses even the brilliant and ebullient Joe Alioto. But unlike Alioto, Brown was not born into a San Francisco family. An African American, Brown was born in Mineola, Texas. His mother sent him as a young teenager to live with his Uncle Itzie in San Francisco. Over lunch at the

Good Food, Fun, and All Business

John Canepa (head chef, 1982–1996): "In the restaurant business, you have to be serious, and Tadich Grill has always been serious. It is a very good, very solid business. A lot of places are Mickey Mouse, where not even the employees respect the place. Here, not the cook, not the dishwasher, not the boss, nobody steals anything from Tadich Grill. When I came here fourteen years ago, I thought, this is a very serious operation, and I like that."

Tadich, Brown told me, "Itzie died two months ago, in August [of 1997], ninety-two years of age. The day I arrived in San Francisco from Mineola, Texas, was August 4, 1951, to be exact." [3]

Asked about his favorite San Francisco restaurants, Brown first mentioned the North Beach Restaurant, run by Lorenzo Petrone and Bruno Orsi.

> I usually eat dinner late, around 9:30, and often alone, and there aren't many quality restaurants open at that hour. The North Beach is one. But there are another dozen restaurants I show up at—Le Central; Perry's; Hayes Street Grill; Powell's Place, which is up on Hayes Street; Stars, which is everybody's standard; Postrio. I do Farallon; I do One Market; I do Boulevard; I do Harry Denton's joints; I do Alioto's on the Wharf; I do the Waterfront Restaurant, the Franciscan, Castagnola's occasionally, Tommaso's on Sundays—that's my Sunday restaurant.

Hearing this, and knowing how fit Willie Brown always looks, I had to ask him when he finds time to work out. He laughed—cackled is closer—in his maniacal way, "Fortunately for me, I am blessed with a good metabolism, and it comes from genes. I am still plannin' to work out. I haven't started it yet, but I've been plannin' it for sixty years.

Getting back to restaurants, Brown went on,

> Mind you, I only eat out. Breakfast every day at the Inn at the Opera, or at Campton Place. For dinner, for really special occasions, I do Fleur de Lys. For *business* special occasions, I do Aqua. And when I *really* want to show people the flavor of San Francisco, which is about once or twice a month, I do Tadich's. Herb Caen brought me here [to Tadich's] in 1963 or 1964. I was first elected to the legislature in 1964.

He and I lunched together almost every week thereafter, until his death. He literally introduced me to his San Francisco. And Tadich's was a weekly spot for Herb Caen. His column was based upon his daily exposure to the life of this city. He went to the places where the life of the city evidenced itself, and Tadich's was one of the places. So he brought me to Tadich's; he took me to Sam's, to Oreste's, Bardelli's, the English Grill at the St. Francis, Vanessi's, Original Joe's, Tommaso's. I got my restaurant education through my friendship with Herb Caen.

As Brown began his remarkable rise in California politics, the Tadich became more than just a place to be seen with San Francisco's most famous columnist. Brown recalled,

> Phil Burton, the legendary congressman, used Tadich's as his headquarters for the brief periods of time that he was in San Francisco. This was where he laid down the rules as to why, for example, we should support Art Agnos when he was running for state assembly. Agnos was a social worker at the time. It was here, at Tadich Grill, that we had many of our meetings. Phil was head of our political operation.

The 1978 passage of Proposition 13 by the voters of California was the high-water mark of a stormy taxpayer's revolt in the state. The chief protagonist of that revolt was a man named Howard Jarvis. Shortly after the passage of Prop 13, Jarvis happened to be in San Francisco, and he entered Tadich at something past noon—when the wait for a table was usually just short of an hour.

Tadich's is strictly a first-come, first-served, no-reservations place of business. And everyone knows it. When, on a blue moon, the

Here Today Gone Today

★ ★ ★

"I'D LIKE to lunch at some place that's typically old San Francisco," said the Baron Philippe de Rothschild last week to his good friend, Art Dealer Bill Pearson — so Bill took him to Tadich's, which, being typically old San Francisco, doesn't take reservations. After they'd waited 30 minutes in the crowded little bar area, the Baron sighed: "I dislike doing things like this, but perhaps it would help if you told them who I am" . . . "I dislike telling you this," grinned Bill, "but I did—15 minutes ago!"

★ ★ ★

IT ALSO seems typically San Francisco that Tadich's. in the financial district, served the Baron fresh shrimp and fresh sand dabs, whereas the next day, lunching at Fisherman's Wharf, he was served shrimp and abalone — both frozen . . . Naturally, much of the conversation was devoted to wine, for Baron Philippe produces Mouton Rothschild, one of France's noblest Bordeaux. "When you have a good wine," he was saying, "it is not enough to decant it. You must also STRAIN it. We tried all kinds of filters, finally discovering that the best is the cheap rayon used in the slips worn by the prostitutes of Paris" . . . "And how did you find that out?" he was asked. "My dear fellow," he shrugged, "we had 20 men working on this project for 20 years — it was inevitable!"

★ ★ ★

■ Herb Caen's column from February 17, 1970.

rules are bent at the Tadich, it is with the greatest and most unseeable discretion. On this occasion, however, Jarvis was taken conspicuously, ostentatiously even, ahead of everyone in line to a table—and to the wild applause of both the seated customers and those still standing in line.

Although Jarvis was a longtime Tadich customer, he had never previously met his host for lunch that day, *Chronicle* columnist Herb Caen, who had vigorously opposed Proposition 13. They were introduced to each other by Steve Buich and were seated with their guests in a private booth. When the waiter arrived with complimentary appetizers and wine, Caen summoned Buich to the table and asked why *he* didn't get that kind of treatment. Steve replied, "Because you haven't lowered my taxes!" Caen's column the next day was devoted to Howard Jarvis and Tadich Grill.

In addition to politics, Tadich's was also the site of physical displays of prowess. Jack LaLanne, an original San Francisco purveyor of physical fitness, one spring afternoon was challenged in Tadich's by a young ex-Marine to a pushup contest. LaLanne accepted the challenge—after a protracted lunch where much wine flowed—and promptly whipped the youngster, performing the exhibit in the middle of the dining room floor. Witnesses remember only that they lost count somewhere after 100.

The list of distinguished guests at the Tadich is too long to relate here, but some are worth mentioning. In 1849, many hardy souls making their way to or from the gold fields ate there. Few of these Argonauts found a golden fleece (and none then signed the Tadich guest register), though in the mining camps more than a few were fleeced. A hundred and forty-three years later, on September 10, 1992, Georgy M. Grechko dined at the restaurant. The famous Soviet cosmonaut signed the restaurant's guestbook, describing his occupation as "astronaut."

John Tadich himself dined at the restaurant on January 8, 1949, and was the first to sign a guestbook, followed by his daughter Mabel Tadich Reedy, that began in that year of the restaurant's hundredth anniversary. The guestbook grew to include the signatures of guests from then on. D. J. Tadich, son of John Tadich, dined at the restaurant on March 10, 1949, as have other Tadiches from various parts of the world. It is unknown what, if any, relation

Guests

DATE	NAME	ADDRESS
Jan. 8-49	John V. Tadich	1327-4ᵗʰ Ave. San Francisco

they have to John Tadich. Milton Duffy signed in on October 16, 1950, writing, "Tadich customer since 1914." His signature is followed by those of Ray McCarthy and Earl Warren. Warren, who had been district attorney of Alameda County and attorney general of California, was about to be elected to his third term as governor of California. In 1953, President Eisenhower would appoint him chief justice of the United States Supreme Court.

B. S. Tilden of Oakland dined in the restaurant on October 26, 1950, as did two other gentlemen, who wrote that they had been customers since 1920 and 1932. Then followed the signature of a John M. Demartini, of 1809 Taylor Street, San Francisco, who scratched a ditto mark beneath the word "customer" written by the previous writer and added, "September 16, 1883." If Mr. Demartini meant to indicate that he had been a customer of the restaurant since the Alexander Badlam days (if he were eighty-five in 1950, he had been eighteen in 1883), he is the earliest known patron of the place, save for Badlam and his cronies.

Groucho Marx ate at the Tadich the same day (that is, October 26, 1950, not September 16, 1883).

Bob Hope ate there five years later, on October 17, 1955. As did Lana Turner, a Mr. Clark Gable, and a woman who signed her name, just beneath Gable's. as Kay Sp—with the rest of the name stricken out and a ditto mark under "Gable." This was Gable's new wife, Kay Spreckels, not yet used to writing her married name.

Norman Vincent Peale, thinking positively, dined with an entourage at the Tadich on February 21, 1957, and was a regular customer for many years.

Al "Jazzbeaux" Collins, who died in 1997, was long a popular disc jockey in San Francisco. He ate at the Tadich on January 11, 1961, signing his name with a great flourish and reminding later readers of the guestbook that his radio station of the time, KSFO, which sported such other great personalities as Don Sherwood, was "The World's Greatest!"

Bob St. Clair, all-pro lineman for the San Francisco 49ers and later a San Mateo County supervisor (and one who favors raw meat, not a regular item on the Tadich menu), stopped in on June 29, 1962; he's still a regular customer. A few months later, another regular, Tennessee Ernie Ford, dined at the Tadich.

Cartoonist Jimmy Hatlo, who drew the character Little Iodine, sketched her picture in the guestbook on May 31, 1963. In July, former California Governor Goodwin J. Knight stopped in for a meal, accompanied, ostensibly, by Emperor Haile Selassie of Ethiopia.

When columnist Herb Caen made one of his regular stops at the Tadich on March 5, 1965, he scrawled in the guestbook, "May Tadich's go on forever!"

Gene Siskel and Roger Ebert ate at the Tadich on January 10, 1985. Siskel gave the joint four stars for fish, and Ebert wrote, "What *Casablanca* is to movies . . . you are to fish!" Later that January, Cary Grant stopped in and wrote, after his meal, "'Twill never change; nor should it !!!" Signing the guestbook a few weeks after that, the comedian Tim Conway drew an arrow to Grant's remark and wrote, "Whatever he said."

Boston is the home of the Kennedy family, and the restaurant claiming to be the oldest in the United States (the Union Oyster House). Senator Edward Kennedy lunched at the Tadich on October 3, 1985, and proclaimed, "Boston and San Francisco—the best."

Jerry Brown, the former governor of California, ate at the restaurant on August 1, 1989. When he left he wrote, "*Age quod agis*," and then saw fit to

---

Kitchen Remodeling, Service for Eight Hundred

Steve Buich: "When you serve seven or eight hundred meals a day with only one hundred seats, you need a kitchen where everything's at hand, where steps are few. In 1967, the restaurant designer told me that we could not put refrigerated drawers for meat and fish close to the broiler because of the intense heat. But in 1985, chef John Canepa argued that it could be done. So John designed an undercounter refrigerator unit with a display case on top, right opposite the broiler, the hottest place in the restaurant. We had it made and installed and it works perfectly and has greatly improved our efficiency.

"After that success, I told John that I'd like to move the pantry to a more efficient place, but there was just no room.

"He said, 'What are you talking about? Right here, where this big refrigerator is, there's plenty of room.' So I told him, 'This weekend, if you have nothing to do, draw me what you have in mind on a piece of paper.' When we finished work on Monday, he said, 'Steve, I've got something to show you.' And by God, he had drawn it all out to scale like an architect, and I could see that it would work."

John Canepa: "It was close, but I designed it, and we built it, and it worked like a charm. I had been in a lot of kitchens around the world. I had already worked in Switzerland, France, and Canada. The best kitchen I ever saw was in Montreal, and it was very small. I told Steve that a small kitchen is more efficient, is fast. You don't lose time. In a big kitchen you lose too many steps."

Steve Buich: "Every afternoon when our shifts were over, John and I would go down to the basement where we marked the concrete floor with precisely the dimensions we had in the kitchen for the pantry. Then we cut large cardboard boxes to size, bound it together with duct tape, and one afternoon we had it finished. We said, 'This is it,' and we called the sheet-metal man. We showed him the spot in the kitchen where we wanted the pantry, and he said it was impossible. We said, 'Come on downstairs,' and when he saw the mock-up he said, 'Maybe it can be done. Can I take this down to my shop?' So he took it to the shop, took all the measurements off the model, built it, and it fit like a glove. It too has a display case, refrigerated drawers, and a hand sink. John Canepa is not only a great chef but has a very creative kitchen design ability."

translate his Latin for the reader—"Do what you are doing." News correspondent Sam Donaldson wrote after his meal, "Terrific!"; Terry Bradshaw, the former Pittsburgh Steelers quarterback, "Outstanding!!"; Rush Limbaugh, "Greater than it's [sic] superb reputation!"; Fran Tarkenton, "The best sand dabs ever!"; and Joe Theisman, the former Washington Redskins quarterback, quoting General Douglas MacArthur, "I shall return," and has.

To a San Francisco restaurant with a tradition as venerable as the Tadich's, some guests, though not household names, may be more cherished than others. Mr. and Mrs. Justin Galatoire Frey and Bernard Guste are just such people. Mr. and Mrs. Frey visited Tadich Grill on April 28, 1986, and Mr. Guste on August 14, 1989. Mr. and Mrs. Frey own the famous Galatoire's Restaurant in New Orleans, and Mr. Guste and his family have for many years owned Antoine's Restaurant in New Orleans. (As Tadich Grill, dating from 1849, is San Francisco's oldest restaurant, Antoine's is New Orleans's oldest. It was founded in 1840.) Mary Henderson and the late Sidney Amber are two others. Ms. Henderson, a customer of the Tadich since 1918, signed the guest register on September 9, 1988: "Great—always my favorite." Sidney Amber was for

---

If You Can't Stand the Heat, Redesign the Kitchen

Mike Buich: "We did many things to the restaurant during John Canepa's years as head chef. For one thing, we had to replace all the ranges. They were shot, they were twenty years old. The heat on that line was so intense that new cooks would sometimes quit. The new ranges are Montague, an industry standard, but the top surface is something that most restaurants don't use. It's a solid, cast-iron top. You get maximum heat in all corners of that solid top, as opposed to being limited to a burner here, a burner there. Well, the cast iron radiates tremendous heat, and there was a solid stainless steel shelf two and a half feet above the cooking surface, and that is where they would keep extra pots and so forth. The heat would roll up under that shelf and come right into the cook's face.

"John and I were talking about ways to get rid of that heat, maybe drilling holes through the shelf. Then the idea occurred to him simply to replace the solid shelf with a series of stainless steel bars. So we installed a shelf made of six stainless steel tubes; now the heat is drawn through by the ventilating system, and it cooled down that cooking area remarkably."

many years, until his death in 1996, the oldest living person born in San Francisco. He last visited the restaurant in early 1994.

Then there are the double-take guests, like the gentleman from Moorooduc, Australia, who stopped in on October 26, 1988—Mr. John Tadich.

In 1847, the year before the discovery of gold in California, fewer than five hundred people lived in the little pueblo that would become San Francisco. Two years later, Tadich Grill was founded, and soon followed the gold rush. Or perhaps it was the other way around. Either way, in another twenty

And More Celebrities

Here is a partial list of other famous folks who have broken bread at the Tadich in the past fifteen years or so: Moscow Mayor Voronokov Alekseevitch, Herb Alpert, the Beach Boys, William Bennett, Fred Biletnikoff, Barry Bonds, Victor Borge, David Bowie, Joseph Califano, Johnny Carson, Gary Carter, Lynda Carter, Dwight Clark, Francis Ford Coppola, Roger Craig, Doris Day, Joe DiMaggio, Norman Fell, George Fenneman, Steve Garvey, Phyllis George, Joel Gray, John Havlicek, Lee Iacocca, Rafer Johnson, Stacy Keach, Michael Keaton, Ralph Kiner, Huey Lewis, George Lucas, Karl Malden, Tim McCarver, Brent Musburger, Don Nelson and his wife Miss Joy on their first wedding anniversary (June 27, 1992), Bob Newhart, Jack Nicholson, Joe Paterno, Don "The Snake" Prudhomme, Linda Ronstadt, Andy Rooney, Al Rosen, Arnold Schwarzenegger and Danny DeVito, Arlen Spector, Ken "The Snake" Stabler, Dave Stewart (Oakland A's pitcher), Fay Vincent, Andy Williams, Stevie Wonder, and Fuzzy and Diane Zoeller.

years, San Francisco was well on its way to becoming a world-renowned culinary city. From its humble beginnings, the Tadich flourished through the wild years of the post–Civil War era, into the wilder parts of the late nineteenth century, and on into two more centuries, surviving longer than any other restaurant.

In the first three months of 2002, an assortment of state legislators, former mayors, businesspeople, janitors, artists, and actors, together with sixty thousand other people, ate at Tadich Grill. At the counter, the diverse clientele mingled with all of the others savvy enough not to wait for a table. And they all came to eat for the same reasons—good food overall, the best seafood particularly, properly brusque service, and a tether to a tradition that's as old as the city of San Francisco itself.

Chapter 8

Recipes from Tadich Grill

■ Elbio Alzogaray,
waiter from 1997 to
the present.

TADICH GRILL LENTIL SOUP

Serves 4 to 6

Lentil soup is offered every Wednesday at Tadich Grill and has been for as long as memory endures. This recipe, reduced and adapted for home use, is a bit different from most others, particularly in the penultimate ingredient.

12 cups white or brown chicken stock (pages 159 and 160)
1 pound lentils
1 ham or pork bone (optional)
Salt
Freshly ground black pepper
2 tablespoons olive oil
1 cup finely chopped yellow onion
2 cloves garlic, finely minced
1 teaspoon chopped fresh thyme
1/4 teaspoon ground nutmeg
3 tablespoons white wine vinegar
1/4 cup chopped cilantro

Reserve 1 cup of the stock. Pour the remaining stock into a large soup pot and add the lentils and ham bone. Bring to a gentle boil over medium-high heat and then immediately decrease the heat to low. Cover the pot and simmer for about 1 hour, or until the lentils are soft (longer than you would cook lentils for a side dish).

Discard the ham bone. Working in batches, transfer the mixture to a food processor and purée until smooth. Return the purée to the pot over medium heat and season to taste with salt and pepper.

Place a sauté pan over medium heat. When hot, add the oil. When the oil is hot, add the onion and garlic and sauté for 3 to 4 minutes, until tender. Add the thyme and nutmeg, mix well, then add to the lentil purée. Bring to a simmer for 10 to 15 minutes, adding the reserved stock as needed to attain the desired consistency. Just before serving, stir in the vinegar.

To serve, transfer to warmed bowls and sprinkle with the cilantro.

Coney Island Clam Chowder

Serves 6

Nobody alive remembers when red clam chowder was not offered at the Tadich. This is the version developed by Dominic Ivelich, head chef from 1961, when Mitch Buich retired, until 1966, when he was succeeded by Dave Sokitch.

1 pound live clams, or 2 (6½-ounce) cans clams
6 to 7 tablespoons bacon fat, or ¼ cup unsalted butter
    plus ¼ cup light olive or vegetable oil
2 yellow onions, chopped
1 clove garlic, minced
1 green bell pepper, stemmed, seeded, and chopped
Leaves from 2 or 3 celery stalks, chopped
1 tablespoon minced fresh parsley
Pinch of curry powder
2 cups canned whole tomatoes, with juice
5 cups bottled clam juice
4 cups white wine fish stock, or as needed (page 162)
2 potatoes, finely diced
Salt
¼ teaspoon freshly ground black pepper
Pinch of cayenne pepper

If using live clams in the shell, scrub well, place in a large saucepan, and pour in about ½ inch of water. Place over high heat and steam for 2 to 3 minutes, until the shells open. Discard any clams that do not open. Drain and then shuck the clams, reserving the liquid from the shells. Coarsely chop the meat. (If using canned clams, drain, reserving the liquid, and chop coarsely.)

Place a large soup pot over medium heat. When hot, add the bacon fat. When the fat is hot, add the onions, garlic, bell pepper, celery leaves, parsley, and curry powder and sauté for 3 to 5 minutes, until glossy and golden. Break up the tomatoes and add to the pot. Mix well and then add the reserved clam liquid, the juice from the tomatoes, the clam juice, and enough fish stock to make 8 cups of liquid in all. Add the potatoes.

Increase the heat to medium-high, bring to a gentle boil, then decrease the heat to low and simmer, covered, for 1¹/₂ hours, until the vegetables are tender and the soup is fragrant and flavorful. Add the chopped clams, salt to taste, pepper, and cayenne. Simmer for 20 minutes, until warmed through. Transfer to warmed soup bowls and serve at once.

Head Chefs at Tadich Grill

Since the 1920s there have been but six head chefs at Tadich Grill. Mitch Buich became chef in 1924. His brother Louie shared chef duties with Mitch until 1953. Mitch retired in 1961 and was followed by Dominic Ivelich (who had begun working for John Tadich in 1912). Ivelich retired on January 21, 1966, and was succeeded by David "Garo" Sokitch, who remained until the same date in 1982. Sokitch's successor was John Canepa, and when Canepa retired in 1996, Fritz Braker took over as head chef.

BOSTON OR NEW ENGLAND CLAM CHOWDER

Serves 4

More than fifteen gallons of this classic chowder are made at Tadich Grill every day (a little more than most home cooks require at a time). The white chowder was introduced as a daily menu item sometime in the 1960s.

4 slices bacon or pancetta, coarsely chopped
3 green onions, white and light green parts, chopped; 3 shallots, chopped; or 1 small yellow onion, chopped
1 leek, white and light green parts, very thinly sliced
5 red potatoes, cut into $1/2$-inch cubes
$1/3$ cup chopped green bell pepper
$1/3$ cup sliced celery
4 cloves garlic, crushed
$1^1/_2$ cups cold water
1 cup white wine fish stock (page 162)
1 teaspoon salt
$1/2$ teaspoon freshly ground white pepper
1 teaspoon Worcestershire sauce
2 drops Tabasco sauce
3 ($6^1/_2$-ounce) cans clams, with juice
2 cups heavy cream
1 teaspoon cornstarch
$1/4$ cup béchamel sauce (page 156)
$1/2$ cup dry sherry

Place a large, heavy soup pot over medium heat. When hot, add the bacon and fry for 6 to 8 minutes, until crisp. Transfer to paper towels to drain. Drain off and discard half of the fat in the pot.

Return the bacon to the pot over medium heat and add the onions, leek, potatoes, bell pepper, celery, and garlic. Sauté in the reserved bacon fat for 3 to 4 minutes, until softened and tender. Add the water, stock, salt, pepper, Worcestershire sauce, and Tabasco sauce and stir well. Cover and simmer for 15 minutes, until the potatoes are tender.

Add the clams and their juice, stir well, and then add the cream. Stir in the cornstarch and the béchamel sauce and simmer for another 15 minutes. Just before serving, stir in the sherry. Transfer to warmed soup bowls and serve at once.

■ Mike Buich at his post, 2002.

BOUILLABAISSE PROVENÇALE

Serves 4 to 6

Bouillabaisse is a Provençal dish made of fish cooked in water or white wine flavored with garlic, parsley, saffron, pepper, and bay leaf. According to Larousse Gastronomique, *many say Venus, the goddess of love, prepared this soup for her handsome husband, Vulcan, to induce a sound sleep. Many versions of this classic dish have been served at the Tadich over the past 150 years. This is the current restaurant favorite.*

1/2 cup olive oil
1 cup diced yellow onion
1 cup diced leek, white and light green parts
1/4 teaspoon chopped fresh fennel leaves
1 cup thinly sliced fennel bulb
1/2 cup dry white wine
1 clove
1 bay leaf
1 sprig savory
4 threads saffron
1 pinch fresh thyme
5 cups white wine fish stock (page 162)
3 tomatoes, peeled and diced
1/2 teaspoon salt
Pinch of freshly ground white pepper
3 1/2 pounds fish and shellfish, such as red snapper, halibut,
    salmon, perch, scallops, prawns, clams, and mussels
5 tablespoons unsalted butter, at room temperature
3 cloves garlic, chopped
4 to 6 thick slices sourdough bread
Pernod, for serving
2 to 3 tablespoons chopped fresh parsley, for garnish

Place a large soup pot over medium heat. When hot, add the oil. When the oil is hot, add the onion, leek, fennel leaves, and fennel bulb and sauté for 4 to 6 minutes, until the onion is translucent and the leek and fennel are tender. Add the wine and deglaze the pot, scraping up any browned bits with a wooden spatula.

Place the clove, bay leaf, savory, saffron, and thyme on a small square of cheesecloth and tie up with kitchen twine into a sachet. Add the sachet, stock, tomatoes, salt, and pepper to the pot and simmer for 20 minutes, until the tomatoes are soft and the mixture is fragrant. Remove the spice sachet and discard. Cut the fish into bite-sized chunks. Add the snapper, halibut, salmon, and/or perch to the pot and simmer for 5 minutes, until the fish is white and opaque. Add the scallops and/or prawns and cook for 2 to 4 minutes, until the prawns are pink and the scallops are firm. Add the clams and/or mussels, cover, and cook for 3 to 5 minutes, until the shells open. Discard any clams or mussels that do not open. Decrease the heat to low and keep the soup warm.

In a small bowl, combine the butter and garlic and mix well. Toast the bread, and spread each slice with the garlic butter.

Transfer the bouillabaisse to warmed soup bowls, add 1 to 2 drops of Pernod to each serving, and garnish with the parsley. Serve immediately, accompanied by the garlic bread.

Weapons of the Trade

Fritz Braker: "Knives are the responsibility of each individual cook. When you start a job, you're responsible for bringing your own knives. My favorite manufacturer is Victorinox from Switzerland. Henckels, the German brand, makes an excellent knife, too.

"Every chef should have a few essential knives. Starting with the smallest one, you need a paring knife to cut small vegetables. (Of course you also need a nice peeler.) Then the next-sized knife would be a French knife to cut vegetables, julienne or however you want to cut. The blade size is an individual kind of thing. I would say it should be 8 to 9 inches. You'd need another, longer-bladed French knife to cut steaks.

"Then, of course, you need a fillet knife, to fillet fish. Fillet knives have a flexible blade, that's very important. You also need a de-boner, to de-bone leg of lamb or veal. To slice smoked salmon, you need a knife with a 15- to 20-inch, very flexible blade. That would probably be it. A basic cleaver would also come in handy. And then for bread, maybe a serrated knife."

Cioppino

Serves 4

Cioppino has been a stalwart of the San Francisco culinary tradition since 1849, the year of Tadich Grill's founding. Two years later, 774 ships had been abandoned in Yerba Buena Cove, which has since been filled in and forms the heart of San Francisco's financial district.

A ship abandoned at what is now the intersection of Davis and Pacific became the city's first Italian waterfront restaurant, owned and operated by Signor Giuseppe Bazzuro of Genoa. Among Signor Bazzuro's dishes was a fish stew, very likely the original cioppino, San Francisco's version of bouillabaisse. The fish market in Genoa was called the Chiappa, and in Genovese the word cioppin *means fish stew. Serve this taste of San Francisco with toasted French bread spread with a mixture of butter, garlic, and oregano.*

Sauce

- 1/4 cup olive oil
- 1/4 cup unsalted butter
- 1/2 yellow onion, chopped
- 1/2 celery stalk, chopped
- 1 carrot, chopped
- 1 tablespoon chopped fresh fennel bulb
- 1/2 green bell pepper, chopped
- 1/2 leek, chopped
- 1 (28-ounce) can crushed tomatoes
- 1 tablespoon tomato paste
- 2 cups water
- 1 tablespoon salt
- 1/4 teaspoon freshly ground black pepper
- 1/2 teaspoon minced fresh oregano
- 1/2 teaspoon minced fresh basil
- 1/4 teaspoon minced fresh thyme
- 4 bay leaves
- Pinch of cayenne pepper

Seafood

8 cherrystone clams
$^1/_2$ pound halibut, cut into $^1/_2$ by 2-inch cubes
$^1/_2$ pound swordfish, cut into $^1/_2$ by 2-inch cubes
8 large diver scallops
8 large prawns, peeled and deveined
4 ounces cooked bay or other small shrimp
$^3/_4$ cup crabmeat
Flour, for dusting
$^1/_4$ cup olive oil
$^1/_4$ cup unsalted butter
1 teaspoon finely chopped fresh garlic
1 cup dry white wine
Chopped fresh parsley, for garnish

To prepare the sauce, place a heavy saucepan over medium heat. When hot, add the oil and butter. When the butter is melted, add the onion and sauté for about 1 minute, until softened but not browned. Add the celery, carrot, fennel, bell pepper, and leek. Cook, stirring, for about 5 minutes, until tender. Add the tomatoes, tomato paste, water, salt, pepper, oregano, basil, thyme, bay leaves, and cayenne. Simmer, stirring frequently, for at least 2 hours and up to 4 hours, until reduced and thickened.

To prepare the seafood, scrub the clams well, place in a large saucepan, and pour in about $^1/_2$ inch of water. Place over medium-high heat and steam for about 5 minutes, until the shells open. Discard any clams that do not open.

Dust the halibut, swordfish, scallops, prawns, shrimp, and crab with flour, shaking off any excess.

Place a large soup pot over high heat. When hot, add the oil and butter. When the butter is melted, add the garlic and sauté for about 10 seconds, until aromatic. Add the halibut, swordfish, scallops, prawns, shrimp, and crab and sauté for 4 to 7 minutes, until golden. Sauté in 2 batches, if necessary. Add the wine and cook, stirring, for 1 minute, until reduced slightly.

Add the sauce, stir well, cover the pot, and cook for 7 minutes over low heat, until heated through. Pour into a serving dish, place the clams on top, and sprinkle with parsley. Serve immediately.

Prawns Sauté Chardonnay with Fresh Mushrooms

Serves 2

Head chef John Canepa introduced this dish to the Tadich Grill menu nearly twenty years ago. It is rich, straightforward, and still going strong. Buttered rice and vegetables are great accompaniments.

12 large prawns, preferably fresh, but frozen will do
2 tablespoons flour
7 tablespoons unsalted butter
4 green onions, white and light green parts, very finely chopped
8 mushrooms, thinly sliced
Pinch of salt
Pinch of freshly ground black pepper
Pinch of dried basil, crushed, or 1 small leaf fresh basil,
    finely chopped
1/2 cup chardonnay or dry white wine
1 teaspoon finely chopped fresh parsley
Juice of 1/2 lemon

Peel, butterfly, and devein the prawns (if rinsed in cold water, blot dry). Dust well with the flour.

Melt 4 tablespoons of the butter in a sauté pan over medium heat. When the butter is hot, increase the heat to medium-high, add the prawns, and sauté for 2 minutes, until they begin to turn pink. Immediately add the green onions, mushrooms, salt, pepper, and basil. Stir well and cook for about 2 minutes, until the vegetables are slightly softened. Add the wine and cook for 2 more minutes, until reduced by about one-third. (This is the secret of the sauté.)

Remove the pan from the heat and stir in the remaining 3 tablespoons butter, the parsley, and lemon juice. (The last addition of butter gives the sauce shine and flavor and also thickens it.) Serve immediately.

SEARED AHI TUNA
WITH PINEAPPLE-MANGO SALSA

Serves 6

Marvelously efficient methods of transportation have brought ahi, a warm-water fish, to market in San Francisco. This is the Tadich's current rave ahi dish.

> 1 cup diced fresh mango
> 1 cup diced fresh pineapple
> 1/2 cup finely chopped red onion
> 1/2 cup finely chopped red bell pepper
> 1/4 cup chopped cilantro
> 2 teaspoons sugar
> 1/2 cup dry white wine
> 6 (4- to 6-ounce) ahi fillets
> 1/2 cup lemon butter sauce (page 157)

In a bowl, combine the mango, pineapple, onion, bell pepper, cilantro, sugar, and wine and mix thoroughly. Cover and refrigerate for at least 1 hour to allow the flavors to blend.

Preheat a broiler or grill, or place a grill pan over medium-high heat. Sear the fish on all sides for a total cooking time of 3 to 5 minutes, until rare or medium rare (unless your guests cannot stand pink flesh in fish, in which case, cook a little longer). Transfer to dinner plates, spoon some sauce over each fillet, and top with the salsa.

Sautéing Fish

John Canepa: "Let's talk about sautéing fish. For little fishes like rex sole or sand dabs, I salt the fish and then dredge them in flour. The secret is to have a very hot pan. The flour helps keep the fish from sticking to the pan, but the pan still needs to be very hot. When you lay the fish in the pan, lay it away from you, so that you don't spatter hot oil or wine onto yourself. We used to sauté fish in butter, the French way. Now, mostly because of concerns about cholesterol, we sauté in white wine."

SHRIMP CREOLE

Serves 4 to 6

Today, just as during its formative gold rush years, San Francisco's cookery borrows heavily from other influences—French, Mexican, Croatian, and the Creole and occasionally the Cajun influences of New Orleans. This shrimp creole has been popular at the Tadich for generations, usually served with fluffy cooked rice.

> 6 tablespoons unsalted butter
> 1 cup thinly sliced yellow onion
> 1 cup julienned green bell pepper
> 2 celery stalks, julienned
> 2 cloves garlic, thinly sliced
> 1 bay leaf
> 2 tablespoons sweet paprika
> 2 cups diced fresh tomatoes
> 1 cup tomato juice
> 4 teaspoons Worcestershire sauce
> 4 teaspoons Tabasco sauce or similar Louisiana hot pepper sauce
> 1 1/2 tablespoons cornstarch
> 1/2 cup water
> 2 to 3 pounds fresh shrimp (20 to 24 count), peeled and deveined

Melt 2 tablespoons of the butter in a sauté pan over medium heat. When the butter is hot, add the onion, bell pepper, celery, garlic, and bay leaf and sauté for 1 to 2 minutes. Before the onion becomes transparent, add the paprika, tomatoes, and tomato juice and stir well. Add the Worcestershire sauce and Tabasco and simmer for about 10 minutes, until reduced by about one-quarter and the vegetables begin to wilt.

In a small bowl, combine the cornstarch and water and stir until dissolved. Stir the cornstarch solution into the sauce. Cook, stirring, for about 2 minutes to cook off the raw taste of the cornstarch.

Place a second sauté pan over medium heat and add the remaining 4 table-spoons butter. When the butter is melted, add the shrimp and sauté, stirring constantly, for about 5 minutes, until pink and tender. Pour the sauce over the shrimp and toss to coat well. Transfer to warmed dinner plates and serve immediately.

TADICH GRILL DUNGENESS CRAB CAKES

Makes 8 cakes

The Tadich's crab cakes are perhaps the best in San Francisco. To any doubters, let's have a contest. The judges will be the winners. The recipe has changed over the years, and no one knows for certain when it was first offered on the menu. This is current head chef Fritz Braker's recipe, which is always accompanied by tartar sauce (page 155).

> **1 tablespoon unsalted butter**
> **1 cup finely chopped shallots**
> **1/2 cup finely chopped celery**
> **3 cloves garlic, finely chopped**
> **1 pound Dungeness crabmeat**
> **1 teaspoon finely chopped fresh basil**
> **1 egg**
> **1/4 cup fine dry bread crumbs**
> **2 to 3 tablespoons béchamel sauce (page 156)**
> **Salt**
> **Freshly ground white pepper**
> **1/4 cup olive oil**

Melt the butter in a large sauté pan over medium heat. When the butter is hot, add the shallots, celery, and garlic and sauté for 3 to 4 minutes, until tender. Transfer to a large bowl and allow to cool. Add the crabmeat, basil, egg, 2 tablespoons of the bread crumbs, and just enough béchamel sauce (start with 1 tablespoon) to bind and moisten the mixture. Season to taste with salt and pepper and mix thoroughly.

Line a baking sheet with parchment paper. Divide the crab mixture into 8 portions and form patties about 3 inches in diameter and 1/2 inch thick. Gently coat the crab cakes with the remaining 2 tablespoons bread crumbs, covering each one thoroughly and evenly. Place the cakes on the baking sheet. Cover with plastic wrap and refrigerate for at least 1 hour and up to 5 hours.

Place a large sauté pan over medium heat. When hot, add the oil to heavily coat the bottom of the pan. As soon as the oil is thoroughly heated, carefully add the crab cakes in batches, without crowding the pan. Sauté for 2 minutes on each side, turning once, until light brown. Place on a warmed platter and serve immediately.

Fillet of Sole all'Agro

Serves 3

When then-head chef John Canepa wrote up this long-running recipe twenty years ago, he described it as "a simple and tasty preparation. Many types of fish fillets can be used." No one is quite sure of the meaning of "all'Agro." Perhaps it is a corruption of "allegro." The Tadich serves this dish garnished with lemon slices and with boiled potatoes and vegetables on the side.

6 (4- to 5-ounce) sole fillets
1 tablespoon flour
1 egg, beaten
Pinch of salt
Pinch of freshly ground black pepper
About 1/4 cup olive oil
1/4 cup dry white wine
Juice of 1 lemon
1 tablespoon chopped fresh parsley
1 tablespoon unsalted butter

Place the fillets in a bowl and sprinkle the flour evenly over them. Toss gently to coat evenly. Break the egg into the bowl and season with salt and pepper. Toss gently again (tossing with your hands works well) until mixed thoroughly.

Place a large sauté pan over medium-high heat. When hot, add enough oil to cover the bottom of the pan evenly. When the oil is hot, add 1 fillet and cook for 4 to 5 minutes, until the underside is light golden brown. Turn the fillet over and cook the second side for 2 to 4 minutes, until opaque and firm. Remove any browned or burned particles of flour from the pan and again add oil to cover the bottom of the pan. Repeat with the remaining fillets, transferring them to a warmed serving dish in a very low oven as each is completed.

Drain off the excess oil from the pan. Add the wine and heat for 2 seconds, still over medium-high heat. Stir in the lemon juice, parsley, and butter. Stir or swirl the mixture for 2 to 3 minutes as it foams, until the sauce begins to thicken. Pour the sauce over the fish and serve immediately.

PAN-FRIED SAND DABS OR REX SOLE

Serves 4

From the 1940s until the 1960s, rex sole was the most popular seafood served in San Francisco restaurants. Today, the "king of sole" has been eclipsed in popularity by the similarly sized but blander sand dabs and by the larger but even blander petrale sole. This preparation works equally well with sand dabs or rex sole and goes well with boiled potatoes and tartar sauce.

1 egg
^{1}/$_4$ cup milk
3^1/$_2$ to 4 pounds sand dab or rex sole fillets, skinned
Flour seasoned with salt and pepper, or fine cracker meal
Olive oil, for sautéing
1 lemon, cut into wedges, for garnish
4 small sprigs flat-leaf parsley, for garnish

Combine the egg and milk in a shallow bowl and beat until well mixed. Dip each fillet into the egg mixture, then dredge thoroughly in the seasoned flour, shaking off any excess.

Place a large nonstick sauté pan over medium heat. When hot, pour in enough oil to just coat the bottom of the pan. When the oil is hot, add the fillets in a single layer (you will have to work in batches, adding more oil as necessary), and cook for 4 minutes, or until the underside is golden brown. Turn the fillets over and cook for 4 minutes, or until the second side is golden brown. Transfer to a warmed platter and keep warm in a low oven as they are completed.

To serve, transfer the fillets to individual plates, garnish with lemon wedges and parsley, and serve immediately.

■ Current broiler chef
Romy Mandap has
been with the
restaurant for thirty
years, having started
in 1972.

FISHERMAN'S SAUCE BAKE

Serves 6

This sauce recipe is one of the oldest known Tadich Grill dishes. It dates from 1910. The Buich family gave it to Doris Muscatine in 1960 for use in her book A Cook's Tour of San Francisco, *and it is reprinted here with Doris's and the Tadich's permission.*

^{1}/$_3$ **cup olive oil**

2 or 3 leeks, white and light green parts, finely chopped

1 bunch green onions, white and light green parts, finely chopped

1 (28-ounce) can whole tomatoes, chopped

Salt

Freshly ground black pepper

^{1}/$_2$ **cup white chicken stock or white wine fish stock (pages 159 and 162)**

3 pounds halibut, sea bass, striped bass, or similar white fish, whole, steaks, or fillets

Place a sauté pan over high heat. When hot, add the oil. When the oil is very hot, add the leeks and green onions and sauté for 4 to 5 minutes, until softened. Add the tomatoes and salt and pepper to taste. Decrease the heat to low and cook, stirring occasionally, for 2 hours, until thickened. Add the stock and simmer for 3 to 4 minutes, until warmed through.

Preheat the oven to 400°F. If the fish is whole, score it along the top so that it will absorb the sauce as it cooks.

Cover the bottom of a baking dish large enough to hold all the fish with about 1^1/$_2$ cups of the sauce, and place the fish on top. Cook whole fish for about 40 minutes, steaks or fillets for 10 to 15 minutes, until the flesh flakes with slight pressure from a fork. The meat should be moist but flaky. Pour the remaining sauce (about 2 cups) over the top of the fish, and return to the oven for 5 minutes, until heated through. Serve at once.

TADICH GRILL SEAFOOD CURRY

Serves 4

For those who favor curry dishes (I am, alas, not one of them), this dish is curry heaven. It has been offered as a special on the Tadich menu for nearly a century. It goes well with a side of chutney.

2 tablespoons unsalted butter
1¼ cups finely chopped white onion
3 cloves garlic, finely chopped
1 red apple, peeled and sliced
2 tablespoons curry powder
2¼ teaspoons salt
3/4 cup dry white wine
2 cups white wine fish stock (page 162)
1 tablespoon cornstarch
1/4 cup water
1½ cups heavy cream
3 cups cooked rice
12 ounces cooked bay shrimp
12 ounces Dungeness crabmeat
8 cooked large ocean prawns, peeled and deveined
1/2 cup grated Parmesan cheese

Preheat the oven to 375°F.

Melt the butter in a large sauté pan over medium heat. When the butter is hot, add the onion, garlic, and apple and sauté for 5 to 7 minutes, until the onion is translucent and the garlic and apple are soft. Do not permit the garlic to brown or burn. Add the curry powder and salt, stir well, and cook for about 2 minutes.

Pour in the wine and deglaze the pan, scraping up any browned bits with a wooden spatula. Add the stock and bring to a simmer for 5 minutes. In a small bowl, combine the cornstarch and water and stir until dissolved. Add the cornstarch solution to the pan and simmer for about 3 minutes, until the sauce has thickened slightly and coats the back of a spoon. Add the cream and simmer until reduced to a smooth, firm sauce, about 7 minutes. Pass through a fine-mesh sieve.

Cover the bottom of 4 individual casserole dishes with a thin layer of the sauce. Place 3/4 cup cooked rice in each dish. Divide the shrimp and crabmeat evenly among the 4 casseroles and then place 2 prawns on top of each dish. Cover the seafood with the remaining sauce. Sprinkle the cheese on top and bake for 10 minutes, until the cheese and sauce are bubbling and lightly browned. Serve immediately.

Sautéing and Deglazing

John Canepa: "Whenever you make a sauté, you can deglaze with hot water, you can deglaze with wine, or you can deglaze with brandy. The taste is in the pan. So most people throw away the best of the sauté. I had a cook once who would change the pan after sautéing because he thought it was burnt.

"You should deglaze with a flat spatula or wooden spoon, never steel because it will scratch. When you have cooked a steak, deglaze the pan with a little stock or wine or brandy, and then add a little onion or mushroom or garlic if you like, reduce it, and then pour the sauce over the steak. (Don't cook the steak in the liquid or you will have a Swiss steak, or pot roast.)

"If you want, you can add a little pinch of flour to the pan before deglazing and stir fast, because it can burn—and then you add the liquid and then you have a brown gravy. The French put in so much butter. I think with a little flour, or a little cornstarch, you get a nice thickness and it's better for your cholesterol, for your health."

FILLET OF SOLE MARGUERY

Serves 4 to 6

This rich dish is a classic of French cookery. The great French chef Auguste Escoffier (1847–1935), "the chef of kings and the king of chefs," offers a version of this recipe in his cookbook, The Escoffier Cook Book. *It is even more of a classic in San Francisco's older restaurants, such as Sam's and Jack's. Two different versions are given in Victor Hertzler's* St. Francis Hotel Cook Book, *published in 1919. Here is the recipe that the Tadich uses when it offers this dish.*

> 2 pounds sole fillets
> 1 cup fresh crab leg meat, preferably Dungeness (not Alaskan king)
> 1/2 cup cooked bay shrimp
> 1 cup thinly sliced mushrooms
> 2 shallots, finely chopped
> 1/2 cup dry white wine, such as sauvignon blanc
> 1/2 cup white wine fish stock (page 162) or clam juice
> Salt
> Freshly ground white pepper
> 2 tablespoons unsalted butter
> 2 tablespoons flour
> 1/2 cup heavy cream
> 1 egg

Preheat the oven to 350°F. Butter a 9 by 12-inch baking dish.

Place the fillets in the baking dish. Layer the crabmeat, shrimp, mushrooms, and shallots on top of the fillets. Pour in the wine and stock and season with salt and pepper. Bake for 12 to 15 minutes, or until the flesh flakes with slight pressure from a fork. With a spatula, carefully transfer the seafood to a second baking dish, reserving all of the cooking juices in the first baking dish.

Melt the butter in a sauté pan over medium heat. When the butter is hot, add the flour and whisk constantly for 2 to 3 minutes, allowing the mixture to bubble but not brown, until the raw taste of the flour is cooked out. Immediately pour in the reserved cooking juices and the cream. Continue to whisk until the sauce thickens and bubbles slightly. Remove from the heat and season to taste with salt and pepper.

Preheat the broiler.

Place the egg in a small bowl and beat well with a fork. One at a time, add 4 tablespoons of the sauce to the egg, mixing thoroughly after each addition. Slowly pour the egg mixture back into the pan with the remaining sauce, whisking constantly. Place the pan back over medium heat and continue to whisk for about 2 minutes, until it just comes to a simmer. Taste and adjust the seasoning with salt and pepper if necessary.

Pour the sauce over the seafood and place under the broiler for 1 to 2 minutes, until bubbling and slightly browned. Serve immediately.

Fish without Fishiness?

John Canepa: "Some people are surprised that we serve so much fish, but the restaurant doesn't smelly fishy. . . . Fish doesn't stink if it's fresh. If you know how to keep it, fish will keep fresh for a few days. The secrets are, first, fresh fish; second, good refrigeration—32 to 35 degrees, at 30 it starts to freeze; and third, you have to keep it elevated, up out of its juices. If it's lying in its juices, it will go bad fast. Very few people know this. Some fish, like sand dabs, rex sole, and petrale, is slimy when it's fresh. If there's no slime, it's old. We buy our fish from three or four different suppliers; that way you can check the availability, the quality, and the prices."

Mike Buich: "We order almost enough fish for each day, so that by the end of the evening we're running out of many items. Now that might make some customers angry, if we don't have what they want late in the evening, but the fish will be back in fresh the next morning. A fish that has been at Tadich Grill two days is, well, a miscalculation. While some fish will keep for a few days, some, like sand dabs, just won't keep at all. That's one of the reasons you don't find them in fish markets very often, and not in some restaurants either."

CRAB AND PRAWNS À LA MONZA

Serves 4

Mitch Buich, head chef at Tadich Grill from 1924 until his retirement in 1961, invented this longtime favorite. It appears on a 1942 menu but undoubtedly was being served long before then. No one is quite sure what "Monza" refers to.

1 tablespoon extra virgin olive oil

1 cup diced fresh mushrooms

1/2 green bell pepper, cut crosswise into 1/4-inch slices

1 cup béchamel sauce (page 156)

2 tablespoons sweet paprika

2 tablespoons dry sherry

Salt

Pinch of cayenne pepper (optional)

2 cups cooked white rice

1 pound crabmeat

4 large (or 8 medium) prawns, shelled and deveined

Preheat the oven to 400°F.

Place a sauté pan over medium heat. When hot, add the oil. When the oil is hot, add the mushrooms, stir quickly, and sauté for 4 minutes, until softened. Remove from the heat and allow to cool.

Bring a saucepan full of water to a boil over high heat. Add the bell pepper and blanch for about 1 minute, until the color brightens. Drain immediately and immerse in a bowl of very cold water for about 2 minutes. Drain again and allow to cool. In a bowl, combine the mushrooms, bell pepper, béchamel sauce, paprika, sherry, salt to taste, and cayenne and mix well.

Cover the bottom of 4 individual casserole dishes with a thin layer of the sauce. Add 1/2 cup cooked rice to one half and 3/4 cup crab to the other half, and place 1 prawn (or 2 medium prawns) on top of the crab. Cover with the remaining sauce and bake for 15 minutes, until bubbling and heated through and the prawns are cooked. Serve immediately.

BAKED AVOCADO AND SHRIMP DIABLO WITH RICE

Serves 4

This recipe was introduced to the Tadich Grill menu in 1973 by then-head chef Dave Sokitch. It has been a mainstay ever since. Notwithstanding the word diablo—*"devil" in Spanish—this baked dish is not at all hot, in the pepper sense, that is.*

2 cups water

1/2 teaspoon salt

1 cup raw long-grain white rice

2 avocados

2 tablespoons unsalted butter

1 tablespoon chopped yellow onion

1 tablespoon chopped green bell pepper

1 tablespoon chopped celery

1/2 teaspoon dry mustard

1/4 cup heavy cream

2 tablespoons dry sherry

Pinch of salt

Pinch of freshly ground black pepper

Pinch of ground nutmeg

1 cup cooked bay shrimp

2 slices Monterey jack cheese

4 mushroom caps

In a saucepan, bring the water and salt to a boil over high heat. Add the rice, stir once, decrease the heat to low, and cover. Cook for 20 to 25 minutes, until the water has evaporated and the rice is tender.

Preheat the oven to 350°F. Butter 4 individual au gratin dishes.

Halve each avocado lengthwise and remove the pits. Scoop out the pulp, dice it, and place in a small bowl.

Melt the butter in a sauté pan over medium heat. When the butter is hot, add the onion, bell pepper, and celery and sauté for 3 to 4 minutes, until softened but not browned. Transfer to a bowl. Add the mustard, cream, sherry, salt, pepper, and nutmeg and mix well. Add the diced avocado and shrimp and mix gently.

Divide the rice among the prepared au gratin dishes. Mound the avocado mixture on top of the rice in each dish, dividing equally. Top each dish with half a slice of cheese and a mushroom cap. Bake for 5 to 10 minutes, until the cheese is melted. Serve immediately.

New Dishes at the Tadich

Fritz Braker: "Mike and I are in agreement: it's very important that we serve our customers their fish speedily, especially during lunch. If we were to add a lot of things to our menu, not only would we have to carry more items, which is the last thing we need, the whole operation would get more complicated, with the result that the food would be slower coming out of the kitchen. So there are no plans to make any great changes on the menu. We play with new dishes through our daily specials.

"I can think about what the special might be the day before, but it's also determined by what the fish sellers have available. I'm on the phone with the fish guys at six or seven in the morning, and they tell me whether they have tuna, mahi-mahi, sea bass, shark, catfish, or salmon. Whatever fish they have available that day is what I usually use for the special.

"I also have a couple of specials with the items that we have on hand. A couple of times a week, as an example, we make a nice seafood brochette. This has swordfish cuts, as well as scallops, prawns, little onions, bell peppers, a couple of mushrooms. Then the sauce. Sometimes I use a nice fresh tomato-basil sauce, or a saffron sauce with fresh chives, or just a lemon vinaigrette sauce with a little basil. I vary it a little bit. Monkfish also appears sometimes as our daily special. We are fortunate, you know, to have all this different seafood available."

OYSTERS ROCKEFELLER

Serves 6

Oysters Rockefeller was invented at Antoine's Restaurant in New Orleans 100 years ago. (Antoine's, founded in 1840 and New Orleans's oldest restaurant, predates the Tadich by only nine years.) Antoine's won't give out its recipe, but the Tadich is willing to share its.

36 large oysters
4 cups rock salt
1 1/2 cups tightly packed fresh spinach
3/4 cup fresh parsley leaves
3/4 cup chopped green onion, white and green parts
6 shallots, coarsely chopped
3 tablespoons chopped fresh fennel leaves
3/4 cup unsalted butter
2 tablespoons anchovy paste
Tabasco sauce
1 cup fresh bread crumbs
1/4 cup Pernod or Ricard
Salt
Freshly ground black pepper

Preheat the oven to 450°F.

Shuck the oysters, straining and reserving the liquid. Scrub and dry the deep halves of the shells, discarding the shallow halves. Pour the rock salt into large baking dishes and arrange the shells on top. Place 1 oyster in each shell.

Combine the spinach, parsley, green onion, shallots, and fennel in a food processor and process until uniformly chopped. Place a sauté pan over low heat. When warm, add the butter. When the butter is melted, add the vegetable mixture and sauté for 5 minutes, until tender. Stir in the anchovy paste, several dashes of Tabasco sauce, and the bread crumbs. Cook, stirring, for 2 to 3 minutes, until well mixed and thick. Add the reserved oyster liquid or more bread crumbs to adjust the thickness. Add the Pernod and salt and pepper to taste (and more Tabasco sauce if preferred) and stir well. Spoon the sauce onto the oysters and bake for about 5 minutes, until the oysters are plump and the sauce is heated through. Serve at once.

OYSTERS KIRKPATRICK

Serves 6

New Orleans has its oysters Rockefeller; San Francisco has its oysters Kirkpatrick, named by its creator, Ernest Arbogast, chef de cuisine for the Palace Hotel, for the hotel's general manager, Col. John C. Kirkpatrick. Kirkpatrick was already well rewarded. He was paid, in those pre-earthquake days, more than thirty thousand dollars a year to manage the hotel. Tadich's version is true to Arbogast's original recipe.

> 4 slices bacon or pancetta
> 5 tablespoons unsalted butter
> 36 large oysters
> 4 cups rock salt
> 1/4 cup ketchup
> 1/2 cup finely minced green bell pepper
> 1/3 cup grated Parmesan cheese

Place a nonstick sauté pan over medium heat. When hot, add the bacon and fry for 6 to 8 minutes, until crisp. Transfer to paper towels to drain, then crumble.

In a sauté pan, melt the butter over medium-low heat without stirring. When completely melted, decrease the heat to low and simmer for 5 minutes. Skim the white foam off the top. Pass through a fine-mesh sieve, reserving the clear yellow liquid and discarding the remainder. The result is clarified butter.

Preheat the oven to 450°F.

Shuck the oysters, straining and reserving the liquid. Scrub and dry the deep halves of the shells, discarding the shallow halves. Pour the rock salt into large baking dishes and arrange the shells on top. Place 1 oyster in each shell. Sprinkle the oysters with the bacon. In a bowl, combine the reserved oyster liquid, clarified butter, ketchup, and bell pepper and mix well. Pour equal amounts over the oysters. Sprinkle the top of each with the cheese.

Bake for 5 for 7 minutes, until browned. (They can be finished off in the broiler if not nicely browned after baking.) Serve immediately.

HANGTOWN FRY

Serves 1

The Hangtown Fry has been a San Francisco favorite for almost as long as the Tadich has been in existence. Reputedly a condemned man's last meal, its story is told in chapter 2. Over the decades, restaurants have developed their own versions, all sharing three key ingredients—eggs, bacon, and oysters. The Tadich's Hangtown Fry is more of a frittata than a scramble.

2 slices bacon
$^1/_2$ cup fine seasoned bread crumbs, toasted, or flour seasoned
    with salt and pepper
6 oysters, shucked
1 tablespoon unsalted butter
3 eggs, lightly beaten
3 or 4 dashes Tabasco sauce
Kosher salt
Freshly ground black pepper

Place a nonstick sauté pan over medium heat. Add the bacon and fry for 6 to 8 minutes, until crisp. Transfer to paper towels to drain.

Place the bread crumbs in a small bowl. Dredge the oysters in the bread crumbs, shaking off any excess.

Pour the bacon fat out of the sauté pan. Add the butter to the pan and melt over medium heat. Add the oysters and sauté for about $1^1/_2$ minutes on each side, or until they just plump up. Crumble the bacon and toss it with the oysters. Pour the eggs into the pan. Season with Tabasco sauce, salt, and pepper to taste, and cook for about 3 minutes, until the eggs are almost set, lifting the edges of the cooked eggs to let the uncooked eggs run underneath.

Carefully flip the frittata over and cook for about 2 minutes longer, or until the second side is set. Transfer to a plate and serve immediately.

CRACKED CRAB WITH MAYONNAISE

Serves 4

There is no more traditional San Francisco Christmas lunch or Christmas Eve dinner than fresh cracked crab with mayonnaise. Pretty simple. You can stir some Dijon mustard into the mayonnaise, or you can substitute hollandaise sauce. Serve with California sauvignon blanc, pinot gris, viognier, or, in a pinch, chardonnay. Remember, crab season comes only twice a year. If you're squeamish about preparing live crab, many fish sellers and grocery stores sell fresh crab already cooked, cleaned, and even cracked.

4 (2¹/₂- to 3¹/₂-pound) live Dungeness crabs
Mayonnaise
Lemon quarters

Bring a very large pot full of salted water to a boil over high heat. Plunge the crabs into the water and boil for about 8 minutes per pound, using the weight of just one of the crabs. (That is, if the crabs are 3 pounds apiece, and you cook 2 at a time, cook for 24 minutes, not 48!) Remove from the water, allow to cool, and drain off any excess water.

Separate the legs from the body and slice the body into quarters along the lines of the leg joints. Remove the dangling intestinal parts and rinse the body under cold running water to remove the so-called "butter." With a meat mallet or the back of a cleaver, crack the large claw pieces slightly, to make it easier to extract the meat. Arrange the crab pieces on a bed of cracked ice, and serve with mayonnaise and lemon. Use a pick, small fork, or claw tip to extract the meat from the shells.

LOBSTER THERMIDOR

Serves 2

This traditional baked dish has been an anchor on the menu for decades. Its popularity waxes and wanes with the availability and price of the main character. The Tadich often offers a crab and lobster thermidor as well.

2 (2-pound) live lobsters
Salt
Freshly ground black pepper
$^1/_4$ cup olive oil
1 cup dry white wine
1 cup white wine fish stock (page 162)
1 tablespoon chopped green onion
2 tablespoons chopped fresh tarragon, or 2 teaspoons dried tarragon
2 cups rich cream sauce (page 157)
1 teaspoon dry mustard
Grated Parmesan cheese
Melted unsalted butter, for drizzling

Bring a very large pot of salted water to a boil over high heat. Plunge the lobsters into the water. The addition of the lobsters will cause the water to stop boiling. When it comes back to a boil, cook the lobsters for 5 minutes for their first pound of weight and 3 minutes for each additional pound, using the weight of just one of the lobsters. (Do not double the cooking time per pound even if you are cooking both lobsters at the same time.) Drain well.

(Alternatively—this method is not for the squeamish—place the live lobsters on a table and, using a heavy, sharp knife and mallet, insert the point of the knife between the body and the tail shell and drive it through to sever the spinal cord.)

Turn the lobster over on its back and split it lengthwise from head to tail, cutting it into 2 parts. (Do not cut through the tail shell.) Remove the stomach and intestinal tract, but leave the roe or "coral," if there is any.

Preheat the oven to 425°F. Place the lobsters in a large baking dish. Season with salt and pepper and brush with olive oil.

Bake, basting frequently with additional olive oil, for 15 minutes, or until the meat is opaque and just firm to the touch. Remove from the oven and allow to cool.

When cool enough to handle, remove the meat from the shells, reserving the shells. Crack the claws and extract the meat. Dice all the lobster meat.

Preheat the broiler. Place the reserved lobster shells on a broiler pan.

Place a sauté pan over medium heat. Add the wine, stock, onion, and tarragon. Cook the mixture down rapidly for 4 to 5 minutes, until it is reduced and slightly thickened. Add the cream sauce, stir well, and heat through for about 3 minutes. Stir in the mustard, taste, and adjust the seasoning with salt and pepper, if necessary. Add the lobster meat, stir well, and heat through for another 2 to 3 minutes. Heap the mixture into the lobster shells. Sprinkle the tops with Parmesan cheese and drizzle with melted butter. Place under the broiler for about 1 minute, or until lightly browned. Serve at once.

TADICH GRILL

CHICKEN OREGANO

Serves 4 to 6

Former mayor Joseph L. Alioto had, to my knowledge, only one criticism of Tadich Grill, one of his favorite restaurants. That complaint was that the restaurant did not serve a dish he called "clams oregano." But it occasionally serves chicken oregano, in this fashion.

> 1¹/₄ cups unsalted butter, or 1 cup olive oil plus ¹/₄ cup
>   unsalted butter
> 3 whole boneless, skinless chicken breasts
> Salt
> Freshly ground black pepper
> Flour, for dredging
> 3/4 cup dry white wine
> 3/4 cup brown veal stock (page 163)
> 2 tablespoons chopped fresh oregano

In a sauté pan, melt 1 cup of the butter over medium-low heat without stirring. (If using olive oil, skip this step.) When completely melted, decrease the heat to low and simmer for 5 minutes. Skim the white foam off the top. Pass through a fine-mesh sieve, reserving the clear yellow liquid and discarding the remainder. The result is clarified butter.

Cut the chicken breasts in half. One at a time, place the breast halves between 2 pieces of parchment or waxed paper. Pound firmly with a meat mallet or the side of a cleaver until about ¹/₄ inch thick. Season with salt and pepper, and then dredge in flour, shaking off any excess.

Place a large heavy sauté pan over medium heat, and add 2 to 3 tablespoons of the clarified butter or olive oil. When the butter is hot, add 2 pieces of chicken and sauté, turning once, for 2 minutes on each side, or until just lightly browned. Replenish the clarified butter and repeat with the remaining chicken. Transfer the chicken to a warmed serving platter as each piece is done.

Drain the excess butter from the sauté pan and deglaze with the wine and veal stock, scraping up any browned bits with a wooden spatula. Simmer over medium-high heat for 2 to 3 minutes, until the liquid is reduced by half. Add the oregano and simmer for 1 minute. Cut the remaining ¹/₄ cup butter into pieces and whisk into the sauce until it is just melted. Taste and adjust the seasoning with salt and pepper if necessary. Pour the sauce over the chicken, and serve immediately.

BOEUF BOURGUIGNONNE À LA TADICH

Serves 4 to 6

John Canepa, head chef at Tadich Grill from 1982 until 1996, took two first prizes at the California Restaurant Association's Culinary Exposition held in 1965 in San Francisco. This is his prize-winning recipe for the classic Burgundy beef dish, served at Tadich Grill on special occasions.

> 2 pounds lean stewing beef, cut into chunks
> 1/4 cup unsalted butter
> 3 yellow onions, finely chopped
> 2 tablespoons flour
> 1 cup red Burgundy wine
> 1 cup brown veal stock (page 163)
> 1 shallot, chopped
> 1/2 teaspoon chopped fresh thyme, or 1/4 teaspoon dried thyme
> 1/2 teaspoon chopped fresh parsley, or 1/4 teaspoon dried parsley
> 1 bay leaf
> Salt
> Freshly ground black pepper

Pat the beef pieces dry and set aside in a bowl. Melt the butter in a large stockpot over medium heat. When the butter is hot, increase the heat to medium-high and add the meat and onions. Cook, turning the meat frequently, for 6 to 8 minutes, until the meat is well seared and browned on all sides. Transfer the meat to a bowl.

Decrease the heat to medium-low and sprinkle the flour over the onions in the pot. Stir well to coat the onions with the flour and meat drippings. Increase the heat to medium and add the wine, stock, shallot, thyme, parsley, bay leaf, and salt and pepper to taste. Stir well to incorporate all of the ingredients. Return the meat to the pot, cover, and simmer over very low heat for 3 hours, until the beef is tender and the sauce has thickened. Serve immediately.

Keeping Cooked Vegetables Fresh

Fritz Braker: "The vegetable of the day, at least twice a week, is beautiful, nice, fresh Blue Lake green beans. Romy, my assistant, cleans the beans at night. Then in the morning we steam them for maybe 3 minutes and then we put them in ice cold water, literally ice cold water with some ice in it, shocking ice cold, and then they stay a beautiful green. See, if you just take them out of the steamer and you let them lie there, they turn brown and ugly. But for all the green vegetables—broccoli, spinach, green beans, chard, Brussels sprouts—it's the same procedure. You steam or cook them in salt water, strain them, and then dump them in ice cold water and totally cool them down. Then you drain them and soak them in a bowl of water with a little garlic, salt, and pepper, however you want it. Then you reheat or sauté them. But, needless to say, the most important thing is, don't overcook them. It is very important that the vegetable be al dente, so there's a bite to it."

■ Romy Mandap prepping for lunch.

CORNED BEEF HASH

Serves 4

Tadich Grill is known principally as a fish house. It is less well known for its traditional, unadorned but equally delicious meat and variety-meat dishes, such as calf liver and onions, boiled beef tongue with Madeira sauce, steaks, and chops. Many of the restaurant's regulars couldn't care less about its fish dishes and come instead for the meat.

3 potatoes, peeled
1 pound cooked corned beef, coarsely chopped
1 small yellow or white onion, chopped
1/2 teaspoon salt
1/2 teaspoon freshly ground black pepper
Pinch of ground ginger
Pinch of ground allspice
1/4 cup vegetable oil
Water or heavy cream, heated
1 tablespoon distilled white vinegar (optional)
4 eggs (optional)

Place the potatoes in a saucepan and add salted water to cover. Place over high heat, bring to a boil, and cook for 20 to 25 minutes, until tender. Drain and allow to cool. When cool enough to handle, coarsely chop the potatoes.

In a bowl, combine the potatoes, corned beef, and onion and stir to mix evenly. Season with the salt, pepper, ginger, and allspice. Place a well-seasoned cast-iron skillet or nonstick sauté pan over medium-high heat. When hot, add the oil. When the oil is hot, add the hash and press it down with a spatula. Let the hash cook slowly, mixing as needed, pressing down and turning after about 5 minutes. Cook the hash for 15 to 20 minutes longer, adding a little water occasionally and letting it cook dry beneath the hash to create a nice crust on the bottom.

Pour about 3 inches of water into a large saucepan over medium-high heat. Add the vinegar and bring to a steady simmer. Crack the eggs into 4 individual cups and slide them one by one into the water. Keeping the water just below a simmer, cook for 3 to 4 minutes, until the whites are set. (If an egg sinks to the bottom of the pan, wait to move it until it is almost set.) Remove the eggs with a slotted spoon, allowing each to drain well. Turn the hash onto a warmed serving dish and top with the poached eggs before serving.

Tadich's Baked Apples

Serves 4

The Tadich offers only a handful of desserts, two being traditional favorites—baked apples and rice custard pudding. Neither would win an award for excellence in haute or nouvelle cuisine, but each remains remarkably popular after more than 100 years on the menu.

4 Red Delicious apples (Golden Delicious, Granny Smiths,
  Winesaps, or other fresh apples can be substituted)
$^1/_2$ cup sugar
$^1/_4$ cup unsalted butter

Preheat the oven to 350°F.

Wash and core the apples, and peel off about 1 inch of skin around the tops. Place the apples upright in a baking dish. Fill each core with about 2 tablespoons sugar and top with 1 tablespoon butter. Pour water into the dish to a depth of $^1/_2$ inch. Bake, basting frequently, for about 30 minutes, or until tender. Serve at once.

RICE CUSTARD PUDDING

Serves 6

Rice custard pudding completes Tadich Grill's most popular dessert duo (along with baked apples). Robert Hass, former poet laureate of the United States, very publicly (on National Public Radio) recommended Tadich's version to Patrick O'Brian, the great novelist, who had decried the lack of "decent pudding" in America. This is current head chef Fritz Braker's version of the old standby.

2¹/₂ cups cooked white rice
1 cup sugar
1 teaspoon vanilla extract
5 eggs, beaten
2 cups whole milk
Pinch of salt
Ground cinnamon, for serving (optional)

Preheat the oven to 350°F. Butter an 8 by 11-inch baking dish.

In a bowl, combine the rice, ¹/₂ cup of the sugar, and the vanilla and mix well. In a separate bowl, combine the eggs, milk, salt, and the remaining ¹/₂ cup sugar and mix well. Add the rice mixture to the egg mixture and stir well. Pour into the prepared baking dish. Bake for 35 to 40 minutes, until the pudding is set.

Remove from the oven and allow to cool to room temperature. Cover and place in the refrigerator until chilled. Serve cold, sprinkled with cinnamon.

Tartar Sauce

Makes 1¼ cups

The recipe for Tadich Grill's tartar sauce is a well-kept family secret, not at all unlike Antoine's recipe for oysters Rockefeller (page 142). And, just as that recipe is not divulged in Antoine's cookbook, the recipe for Tadich's tartar sauce will remain a secret, at least through the publication of this book. You'll have to visit the restaurant to taste the real deal, but here is a delicious alternate.

> 1 cup mayonnaise, preferably homemade
> 1 tablespoon finely chopped fresh parsley
> 1 tablespoon finely chopped fresh chives
> 1 teaspoon finely chopped fresh tarragon
> 1 tablespoon finely chopped fresh chervil
> 1 tablespoon capers
> 1 teaspoon finely chopped fresh garlic
> 1 small dill pickle, finely chopped

In a bowl, combine all the ingredients, mix well, and refrigerate for at least 1 hour before serving.

The Tadich's Tartar Sauce

Fritz Braker: "We go through gallons and gallons and gallons of the tartar sauce. We buy the mayonnaise but we grind our own vegetables—green onions, parsley, cornichons, gherkins, capers, all the vegetables, everything that goes in it. There's even a little bit of ground boiled potato to give it a firmness. And some salt and pepper and lemon juice. It's an excellent tartar sauce. I like it very much. But I can't tell you the proportions, or the other secrets about it."

BÉCHAMEL SAUCE

Makes 2 cups

Béchamel sauce is a principal ingredient in the Tadich's crab cakes (page 129), as well as in its Crab and Prawns à la Monza (page 138). Here is head chef Fritz Braker's recipe for this essential and classic sauce.

2 cups milk
2 tablespoons unsalted butter
2 tablespoons flour
Salt
Freshly ground white pepper

Place the milk in a saucepan over medium-high heat and bring to a boil. Remove from the heat, allow to cool to room temperature, then cover and refrigerate until chilled.

Place a saucepan over low heat. Add the butter and stir until melted. Add the flour and stir well. When the mixture bubbles, add the chilled milk, a very little at a time, stirring and beating until all the milk has been added and the sauce is thick and creamy. Season to taste with salt and pepper.

LEMON BUTTER SAUCE

Makes 2 cups

This simple sauce is delicious drizzled over ahi fillets, just prior to topping them with a salsa such as the pineapple-mango salsa on page 127. It works just as well on mahi-mahi, ono, and escolar fillets.

> 1 cup unsalted butter
> 1/4 cup sugar
> Juice of 3 lemons (about 1/2 cup)
> 1 tablespoon grated lemon zest

Place a small saucepan over low heat. Add the butter and stir until melted. Add the sugar and stir until dissolved. Stir in the lemon juice and zest, then stir constantly for 2 to 3 minutes, until the sauce begins to thicken. (This sauce can be refrigerated for several days.)

RICH CREAM SAUCE

Makes 1 cup

This basic sauce has many uses. A central ingredient in Lobster Thermidor (page 146), it is richer and thicker than traditional béchamel sauce. For an even thicker sauce, use more flour.

> 2 tablespoons unsalted butter
> 2 tablespoons flour
> 1/2 cup whole milk
> 1/2 cup heavy cream
> Salt
> Freshly ground white pepper

Place a small saucepan over low heat. Add the butter and stir until melted. Add the flour and stir until well blended. Remove the pan from the heat or place over hot water. Slowly add the milk and cream, blending until smooth. Return to low heat and cook slowly, stirring constantly, for 4 to 5 minutes, until thickened and smooth. Season to taste with salt and pepper.

Girard's French Dressing

Makes 1 cup

Girard's French Restaurant operated at 65 Ellis Street until 1890, when the proprietor, Wilfred J. Girard, moved the operation to new quarters. It began bottling its justly famous French dressing in the 1930s. A luscious version of the dressing is offered occasionally at Tadich Grill.

1 egg, beaten
2 teaspoons Dijon mustard, or $^{1}/_{2}$ teaspoon dry mustard
$^{1}/_{2}$ cup chardonnay or champagne vinegar
2 tablespoons extra virgin olive oil
$^{1}/_{4}$ cup water
1 tablespoon finely ground bread crumbs
$^{1}/_{4}$ teaspoon finely minced fresh garlic
$1^{1}/_{2}$ teaspoons sugar
Salt
$^{1}/_{4}$ teaspoon freshly ground white pepper

In a bowl, combine all the ingredients and mix well. Refrigerate (preferably overnight) before serving.

White Chicken Stock

Makes 8 to 12 cups

Chicken stock is the foundation (in French, fonde*) of many sauces and, of course, soups. When the Tadich makes stocks, it makes them in ten- or fifteen-gallon quantities. This is the lighter of the Tadich's two chicken stocks. It is unsalted since the flavoring will be adjusted once the stock is used in a recipe.*

   12 cups water, or as needed
   1 (4-pound) roasting or frying chicken, or 4 to 5 pounds chicken
      parts or bones (necks, backs, wings, breast bones)
   1 yellow onion, whole or halved, pierced with a clove
   1 large celery stalk with leaves
   1 large carrot, peeled
   1/2 green bell pepper (optional)
   3 or 4 whole peppercorns
   1 small bay leaf or Mediterranean bay leaf
   1 tablespoon chopped fresh parsley, or 1 teaspoon dried parsley
   1 teaspoon chopped fresh basil
   1 teaspoon chopped fresh thyme

Bring the water (or enough to just cover the chicken) to a boil over high heat in a large stockpot. Place the chicken in the boiling water and blanch for about 5 minutes. Skim any scum from the surface. Decrease the heat to medium-low. If necessary, add more water to ensure that the chicken is completely covered.

Add the onion, celery, carrot, bell pepper, peppercorns, bay leaf, parsley, basil, and thyme and stir well. Cover and simmer gently, but do not allow to boil. Check the stock every 4 hours and replenish the water as needed, keeping the chicken sufficiently covered. Simmer slowly for at least 8 hours and up to 12 hours.

Remove the stock from the heat and pass through a fine-mesh sieve. Return to the pot. (If you'd like a slightly richer stock, it can be simmered, uncovered, at this point for 40 to 60 minutes.) Allow to cool to room temperature, transfer to smaller containers if necessary, and then refrigerate. After the stock has thoroughly chilled, skim the layer of congealed fat from the surface. This stock will keep for 4 to 5 days in the refrigerator and 3 months in the freezer.

Brown Chicken Stock

Makes 8 to 12 cups

This is the Tadich's darker chicken stock, used when they want a richer flavor or deeper color than the white stock would produce. Like the white stock, it has no added salt.

1 (5-pound) roasting chicken, cut into pieces, or 6 pounds chicken
    parts or bones (necks, backs, wings, breast bones)
2 cups dry white wine
4 quarts water, or as needed
2 yellow onions, each pierced with a clove
2 celery stalks with leaves, halved
2 carrots, peeled and halved
1 green bell pepper, stemmed, seeded, and quartered (optional)
6 peppercorns
1 bay leaf, or 2 Mediterranean bay leaves
1 tablespoon chopped fresh parsley, or 1 teaspoon dried parsley
1 to 2 teaspoons chopped fresh basil
1 to 2 teaspoons chopped fresh thyme

Preheat the oven to 450°F.

Place the chicken in a roasting pan and brown for 40 to 60 minutes. Turn the chicken every 20 minutes to ensure even and thorough roasting. When the juices have caramelized in the pan and the chicken is a rich, golden brown, transfer the chicken to a large stockpot. Pour out any accumulated fat from the roasting pan and place the pan on the stovetop over medium-high heat. Thoroughly deglaze with the wine, scraping up any browned bits with a wooden spatula.

Add the deglazings to the stockpot with the chicken and add the water, or enough to fill the pot more than halfway and completely cover the chicken. Bring to a boil over medium-high heat, and then promptly decrease the heat to low to achieve a simmer. Skim the scum from the surface as it rises. Add the onions, celery, carrots, bell pepper, peppercorns, bay leaf, parsley, basil, and thyme and stir well. Cover the pot and simmer for at least for 8 hours and up to 12 hours. Do not allow to boil. (Uncover the pot and simmer for another 1 to 1 1/2 hours for a richer, more concentrated stock.)

Remove the stock from the heat and pass through a fine-mesh sieve. Return to the pot and allow to cool to room temperature. Transfer to smaller containers if necessary and then refrigerate. After the stock has thoroughly chilled, skim the layer of congealed fat from the surface. This stock will keep for 4 to 5 days in the refrigerator and 3 months in the freezer.

The same directions can be used to make turkey stock (ordinarily not nearly as tasty or as useful in sauces) or other poultry stocks. (A stock made from gamier birds, such as pheasant or goose, should not be simmered nearly as long.)

The Making of Stock— the "Foundation"

John Canepa: "We make four kinds of stock—chicken, fish, beef, veal—at Tadich Grill, and we make them every night, or every other night. They simmer all night long, with bones, onions, carrots, celery, and leeks. Leeks are very important, especially the tough part, the green part. You don't throw away anything. Carrots with their peelings, onions with their peelings. Stocks shouldn't boil; they should only simmer. The fish stock doesn't simmer all night— only an hour or so.

"If you are making a chicken stock, and you want to make a brown stock, brown the bones in the oven or under the broiler. But don't forget to deglaze the broiling pan. The flavor is in the drippings on the bottom of the pan. Deglaze, and put that in the stock pot."

WHITE WINE FISH STOCK

Makes 4 cups

This classic fish stock, or fish fumet, *is the work of Tadich Grill head chef Fritz Braker, who has adapted it for home use. It is the foundation for many recipes used at the Tadich and can usually be used in place of the fish stock or clam juice called for in cookbooks.*

3 tablespoons olive oil
1/3 cup chopped yellow onion
1/3 cup sliced carrot
1/3 cup sliced celery
4 cups white wine
2 pounds white fish bones and bits of fish, with no blood or heads
   (halibut would work, but not salmon)
4 cups water, or as needed
Pinch of dried fennel seed
Pinch of fresh thyme
1 bay leaf
4 sprigs parsley
Salt
Freshly ground white pepper

Place a small stockpot over medium-high heat. When hot, add the oil. When the oil is hot, add the onion, carrot, and celery and sauté for 5 to 7 minutes, until they just begin to brown. Add the wine, fish bones, and enough water to cover the bones by 1 to 2 inches and bring to a boil. Skim the scum from the surface as it rises. Add the fennel, thyme, bay leaf, and parsley and stir well. Decrease the heat to low and simmer for 1 hour. Remove the stock from the heat and strain through cheesecloth. Return to the pot and season with salt and pepper to taste.

Allow to cool to room temperature, about 30 minutes. Transfer to smaller containers if necessary and then refrigerate. This stock will keep for 3 to 4 days in the refrigerator and 3 months in the freezer.

Brown Veal Stock

Makes 12 to 16 cups

This is Tadich Grill head chef Fritz Braker's prized recipe for a meat stock for richer sauces and soups.

    4 to 5 pounds veal bones, cut into pieces
    1/4 cup vegetable oil
    2 carrots, peeled and diced
    1 yellow onion, peeled and diced
    1 large leek, white part only, chopped
    2 celery stalks, including some greens, chopped
    2 cups red wine
    1 1/2 cups canned tomato purée
    6 cloves garlic, crushed
    2 bay leaves
    3 cloves
    Pinch of dried thyme
    Pinch of dried rosemary
    1 teaspoon whole black peppercorns
    12 cups water, or as needed
    Salt

Preheat the oven to 450°F.

Place the bones in a roasting pan and roast for 30 minutes, until browned. Add the oil, carrots, onion, leek, and celery and cook for 30 minutes, until the vegetables are browned. Transfer the bones and vegetables to a large stockpot. Place the roasting pan on the stovetop over medium-high heat and thoroughly deglaze with the wine, scraping up any browned bits with a wooden spatula.

Add the deglazings to the stockpot along with the tomato purée, garlic, bay leaves, cloves, thyme, rosemary, peppercorns, and enough water to cover the bones by 1 to 2 inches. Simmer, uncovered, for at least 8 hours and up to 12 hours. If in the last few hours it looks as though the liquid is evaporating too fast, add more water to compensate. Add salt to taste at the end of cooking.

Remove the stock from the heat and pass through a fine-mesh sieve. Return to the pot and allow to cool to room temperature. Transfer to smaller containers if necessary and then refrigerate. After the stock has thoroughly chilled, skim the layer of congealed fat from the surface. This stock will keep for 4 to 5 days in the refrigerator and 3 months in the freezer.

Notes

Chapter 1

1. John Keats's sonnet "On First Looking into Chapman's Homer" has Cortez, not Balboa discovering the Pacific Ocean. That got me to thinking:

   > "On Second Looking into Chapman's Homer"
   > (An Inca to an Inca, on an
   > Andes ridge gazing west:)

   > That man Keats he thinks
   > Cortez discovered this priceless sea.

   > What a fatuous fool he be.
   > Every Inca boy since Noah
   > Knows it was Balboa.

2. Frank Marryat, *Mountains and Molehills, or Recollections of a Burnt Journal* (London: Longman, Brown, Green and Longmans, 1855), 180–81.

3. John B. McGloin, S.J., *San Francisco: The Story of a City* (San Rafael: Presidio Press, 1978), 68–71

4. Louis K. Loewenstein, *Streets of San Francisco* (San Francisco: Lexikos, 1984), 18.

5. Ibid., 46.

6. "Tadich's Grill," in the Diamond Jubilee edition of *San Francisco News Letter,* 5 September 1925, quoted in Vjekoslav Meler, ed., *The Slavonic Pioneers of California* (San Francisco: The Slavonic Pioneers of California, 1932), 51.

7. McGloin, *San Francisco: The Story of a City,* 27, 247; Loewenstein, *Streets of San Francisco,* 42.

Chapter 2

1. Helen Hunt Jackson, *Ramona* (New York: Grosset & Dunlap, 1884, 1912), 53.

2. Oscar Lewis, *San Francisco: Mission to Metropolis* (Berkeley: Howell-North Books, 1966), 46.

3. McGloin, *San Francisco: The Story of a City,* 32–33.

4. Lewis, *San Francisco: Mission to Metropolis,* 49.

5. James S. Holliday, *The World Rushed In* (New York: Simon and Schuster, 1981), 26.

6. Wallace Stegner, "The Gift of Wilderness," in *One Way to Spell Man* (Garden City, NY: Doubleday & Company, 1982), 164.

7. R. L. Stevenson, *San Francisco: A Modern Cosmopolis* (1882; reprint, San Francisco: Book Club of California, 1963), 19–22.

8. Karl Marx and Friedrich Engels, "Review: January–February 1850," *Neue Rheinische Zeitung Revue* (January–February 1850), reprinted in David Fernbach, ed., *The Penguin Marx Library*, vol. 1, Political Writings (Hardmondsworth, England: Penguin Books, 1973), 265, 275.

9. Lewis, *San Francisco: Mission to Metropolis*, 123, 165. See also Oscar Lewis, *The Big Four* (New York: Alfred A. Knopf, 1938).

10. Lewis, *San Francisco: Mission to Metropolis*, 113, 150–52, 172; McGloin, *San Francisco: The Story of a City*, 97–99.

11. Frank Soulé, John H. Gihon, and James Nesbit, *The Annals of San Francisco* (San Francisco: D. Appleton & Company, 1855), 640.

12. Claude Schopp, *Alexandre Dumas: Genius of Life*, trans. A. J. Koch (New York: Franklin Watts, 1988), 485–90.

13. Katherine Bitting, *Gastronomic Bibliography* (San Francisco: n.p., 1939), 338.

14. Clifton Fadiman, ed., *The Little, Brown Book of Anecdotes* (Boston: Little, Brown & Company, 1985), 177.

15. Noah Brooks, "Restaurant Life in San Francisco," *Overland Monthly* 1 (November 1868): 465, 467.

16. Ibid., 465, 468, 470–71.

17. Doris Muscatine, *Old San Francisco, from Early Days to the Earthquake* (New York: G. P. Putman's Sons, 1975), 229–30, 301–2.

18. Oscar Lewis and Carrol D. Hall, *Bonanza Inn* (New York: Alfred A. Knopf, 1939), 116–200.

Chapter 3

1. John Tadich, "The Jugoslav Colony of San Francisco on My Arrival in 1871," in Meler, *Slavonic Pioneers*, 40.

2. Ibid., 41–42.

3. McGloin, *San Francisco: The Story of a City*, 108–9.

4. Information compiled by Steve L. Buich and Donna Umeki from Kimball's San Francisco Directory, 1850; Parker's San Francisco Directory, 1852; LeCounty & Strong's San Francisco City Directory, 1854; Baggett's San Francisco Business Directory, 1856; San Francisco business tax records, 1850–1856; Colville's San Francisco Directories from 1856 on; Langley's San Francisco Business Directories, 1862–1875; and Bishop's San Francisco City Directories from 1875.

5. Meler, *Slavonic Pioneers*, 51.

6. Louis Stellman, *Sam Brannan: Builder of San Francisco* (New York: Exposition Press, 1954; reprint, Fairfield, CA: James Stevenson Publisher, 1996), 174–237.

7. Meler, *Slavonic Pioneers*, 51.

8. Gladys Hansen and Emmet Condon, *Denial of Disaster: The Untold Story and Photographs of the San Francisco Earthquake and Fire of 1906* (San Francisco: Cameron and Company, 1989); William Bronson, *The Earth Shook, the Sky Burned* (Garden City, NY: Doubleday & Company, 1959).

9. Quoted in Bernard Taper, ed., *Mark Twain's San Francisco* (New York: McGraw-Hill Book Company, 1963), 125.

10. Writers' Program of the Works Progress Administration (WPA) in Northern California, *San Francisco: The Bay and Its Cities*, American Guide Series (New York: Hastings House, 1940), 56–57.

11. The passages quoting John Tadich are all from his 1932 essay in Meler, *The Slavonic Pioneers of California*.

12. The family lived in San Francisco's then relatively new Sunset District, west of Twin Peaks, at 1327 Fourth Avenue.

13. Ruby Tadich Suhr Lawler, interview by author, St. Francis Yacht Club, San Francisco, 8 April 1997.

14. John Van der Zee, *The Gate: The True Story of the Design and Construction of the Golden Gate Bridge* (New York: Simon and Schuster 1986), 158–60.

15. *San Francisco Chronicle* (8 December 1917), 1.

Chapter 4

1. Brooks, "Restaurant Life," 465, 473.

2. Raymond Ewell, *Dining Out in San Francisco and the Bay Area*, 2d ed. (Berkeley: Epicurean Press, 1948), 22–23. A recommended account is Clarence Edwords, *Bohemian San Francisco: Its Restaurants and Their Most Famous Recipes* (San Francisco: Paul Elder and Company, 1914), 21–22.

3. Edwords, *Bohemian San Francisco*, 21–22.

4. Muscatine, *Old San Francisco*, 226–27.

5. Edwords, *Bohemian San Francisco*, 16.

6. Muscatine, *Old San Francisco*, 230.

7. Edwords, *Bohemian San Francisco*, 16.

8. Ibid., 16–17.

9. Lewis and Hall, *Bonanza Inn*, 49.

10. McGloin, *San Francisco: The Story of a City*, 96–102; Gray Brechin, *Imperial San Francisco: Urban Power, Earthly Ruin* (Berkeley: University of California Press, 1999), 89–92.

11. Evelyn Wells, *Champagne Days of San Francisco* (New York: D. Appleton-Century Company, 1939), 26–28.

12. Ibid., 182.

13. Edwords, *Bohemian San Francisco*, 27–29.

14. Ibid., 26.

15. Ibid., 29–30.

16. Ibid., 32.

17. Doris Muscatine, *A Cook's Tour of San Francisco* (New York: Charles Scribner's Sons, 1963), 9.

18. Ibid., 9–10.

19. Oscar Lewis, *Bay Window Bohemia* (Garden City, NY: Doubleday & Company, 1956), 102–3.

20. Albert Parry, *Garrets and Pretenders*, rev. ed. (New York: Dover Publications, 1960), 236.

21. Never mind that the motion picture, done in 1941, shows a silhouetted Bay Bridge, which hadn't been built in 1928, and later-vintage automobiles. See the North Point Press edition of Hammett's *The Maltese Falcon* (San Francisco, 1984), vii–ix, 279–80.

22. Ibid., 208.

23. Herb Caen, column, *San Francisco Chronicle*, 2 June 1963. In *The Best of Herb Caen 1960–1975* (San Francisco: Chronicle Books, 1991), 49–50.

24. Henry Evans, *Bohemian San Francisco* (San Francisco: The Porpoise Bookshop, 1955), 3.

25. WPA, *San Francisco: The Bay and Its Cities*, 243.

26. Herb Caen, column, *San Francisco Chronicle*, 3 April 1963. In *Best of Herb Caen*, 47–48.

27. Herb Caen, *Baghdad by the Bay* (New York: Doubleday & Company, 1949), 173.

28. Among Caen's many columns relating the story, see his 18 January 1989 column, in the *San Francisco Chronicle* and his column of 20 June 1984 in, of all places, the *Honolulu Advertiser*. In his well-known *Baghdad by the Bay* on page 173, Caen told the story more animatedly:

    Another classic North Beach delicacy was invented at New Joe's—an unlikely mishmosh called a "Joe's Special." Its birth was pure accident and invention, fathered by a rising young bandleader named Bunny Burson, who was tragically killed at a Peninsula party shortly after. Bunny walked into Joe's for a hamburger one night, only to be told that not enough hamburger was left for a sandwich.

"So whatcha got back there?" asked Burson.

"Oh," shrugged the cook, looking around, "just a coupla eggs, a little hamburger—and—and—some spinach."

"Fair enough," said Burson. "Mix 'em together and fry it in a little oil."

That was the first "Joe's Special." Now it's featured on the menus of a dozen Italian restaurants by that same name.

29. Herb Caen, column, *San Francisco Chronicle,* 8 July 1971. In *Best of Herb Caen,* 207.

30. WPA, *San Francisco: The Bay and Its Cities,* 243.

31. M. F. K. Fisher, *How to Cook a Wolf* (San Francisco: North Point Press, 1988), 4.

32. M. F. K. Fisher, *To Begin Again* (San Francisco: Pantheon Books, 1992), 110.

33. Alice B. Toklas, *The Alice B. Toklas Cookbook* (New York: Harper & Row, 1954), 134.

Chapter 5

1. Ruby Tadich Suhr Lawler interview.

2. Ibid.

3. *San Francisco Examiner* (28 November 1953), 1.

4. Ewell, *Dining Out in San Francisco,* 55.

5. Leonce Picot, ed., *Restaurants of San Francisco* (Ft. Lauderdale: Gourmet International, 1963), 99.

6. Muscatine, *Cook's Tour,* 140.

7. Loewenstein, *Streets of San Francisco,* 12.

8. Howard C. Gardiner, *In Pursuit of the Golden Dream: Reminiscences of San Francisco and Northern and Southern Mines, 1849–1857,* ed. Dale L. Morgan (Stoughton, MA: Western Hemisphere, Inc., 1970), 164–65.

Chapter 6

1. Jack Kerouac, *On the Road* (New York: New American Library, 1985), 144.

2. Herb Caen, column, *San Francisco Chronicle,* 12 December 1996.

3. Herb Caen, column, *San Francisco Chronicle,* 5 February 1961. In *Best of Herb Caen,* 19–20.

4. Herb Caen, column, *San Francisco Chronicle*, 8 September 1972. In *Best of Herb Caen*, 229–30.

5. Herb Caen, column, *San Francisco Chronicle*, 12 December 1996.

6. Herb Caen, column, *San Francisco Chronicle*, 24 March 1995.

7. Jim Wood, "Chez Panisse," *San Francisco Examiner* (22 August 1991), C-1.

8. Here's how I worked out that ratio. According to the San Francisco Restaurant Association, there are 3,300 restaurant permits outstanding in the city. But those permits include such things as hot dog and pretzel carts. So it's a matter of guesswork as to whether there are 2,500 real restaurants, or 3,000. Either way, there are approximately 750,000 people living in the city, and either long or short division produces the quotient.

9. James Beard Foundation, *Calendar and Newsletter*, June 1997, 8–9.

Chapter 7

1. Patricia Unterman and Stan Sesser, *Restaurants of San Francisco* (San Francisco: Chronicle Books, 1988), 241.

2. Joseph L. Alioto, interview by author, Tadich Grill, 25 April 1997.

3. Willie L. Brown Jr., interview by author, Tadich Grill, 29 October 1997.

BIBLIOGRAPHY

Asbury, Herbert. *The Great Illusion: An Informal History of Prohibition.* New York: Doubleday & Company, 1950.

Berger, Francis de Talavere, and John Parke Gustis. *Sumptuous Dining in Gaslight San Francisco.* New York: Doubleday & Company, 1985.

Bespaloff, Alexis. *The New Frank Schoonmaker Encyclopedia of Wine.* New York: William Morrow and Company, 1988.

Brennan, Ella, and Dick Brennan. *The Commander's Palace New Orleans Cookbook.* New York: Clarkson N. Potter, 1984.

Brennan, Pip, Jimmy Brennan, and Ted Brennan. *Breakfast at Brennan's.* New Orleans: Brennan's, Inc., 1994.

Bronson, William. *The Earth Shook, the Sky Burned.* Garden City, NY: Doubleday & Company, 1959.

Brooks, Noah. "Restaurant Life in San Francisco." *Overland Monthly* 1 (November 1868).

Brown, Helen. *West Coast Cook Book.* New York: Little, Brown & Company, 1952.

Caen, Herb. *Baghdad by the Bay.* New York: Doubleday & Company, 1949.

————. *The Best of Herb Caen 1960–1975.* San Francisco: Chronicle Books, 1991.

Cahill, Thomas. *How the Irish Saved Civilization.* New York: Doubleday, 1995.

Caughey, J. W. *California.* New York: Prentice-Hall, 1940.

Chesterton, G. K. "Water and Wine." In *The Collected Poems of G. K. Chesterton.* New York: Dodd, Mead & Company, 1946.

Davis, William Heath. *Seventy-Five Years in California.* San Francisco: John Howell, 1929.

Dickson, Samuel. *Tales of San Francisco.* Stanford: Stanford University Press, 1957.

Dillon, Richard H. *Embarcadero.* New York: Coward-McCann Inc., 1959.

Dumas, Alexandre. *Dictionary of Cuisine.* Edited, abridged, and translated by Louis Colman from *Le Grand Dictionnaire de Cuisine* (1873). New York: Simon and Schuster, 1958.

Durant, Will, and Ariel Durant. *The Story of Civilization. Vol. I, Our Oriental Heritage.* New York: Simon and Schuster, 1954.

————. *The Story of Civilization. Vol. VII, The Age of Reason Begins.* New York: Simon and Schuster, 1961.

————. *The Story of Civilization. Vol. VIII, The Age of Louis XIV.* New York: Simon and Schuster, 1963.

————. *The Story of Civilization. Vol. X, Rousseau and Revolution.* New York: Simon and Schuster, 1967.

Dwinelle, John W. *The Colonial History of the City of San Francisco.* San Francisco: Towne & Bacon, 1867.

Edwords, Clarence E. *Bohemian San Francisco: Its Restaurants and Their Most Famous Recipes.* San Francisco: Paul Elder and Company, 1914.

Engelhardt, Z. *San Francisco or Mission Dolores.* Chicago: Franciscan Herald Press, 1924.

Evans, Henry. *Bohemian San Francisco.* San Francisco: The Porpoise Bookshop, 1955.

Everett, Marshall. *Complete Story of the San Francisco Earthquake.* Chicago: The Bible House, 1906.

Ewell, Raymond. *Dining Out in San Francisco and the Bay Area,* 2d ed. Berkeley: Epicurean Press, 1948.

Fadiman, Clifton, ed. *The Little, Brown Book of Anecdotes.* Boston: Little, Brown & Company, 1985.

Fisher, M. F. K. *How to Cook a Wolf.* San Francisco: North Point Press, 1988.

————. *To Begin Again.* San Francisco: Pantheon Books, 1992.

Gardiner, Howard C. *In Pursuit of the Golden Dream: Reminiscences of San Francisco and Northern and Southern Mines, 1849–1857,* ed. Dale L. Morgan. Stoughton, MA: Western Hemisphere, Inc., 1970.

Gazi, Stephen. *A History of Croatia.* New York: Philosophical Library, 1973; reprint, New York: Barnes & Noble Books, 1993.

Gilliam, Harold. *San Francisco Bay.* Garden City, NY: Doubleday & Company, 1957.

Gonzmart, Adela Hernandez, and Ferdie Pacheco. *The Columbia Restaurant Spanish Cookbook.* Gainesville: University Press of Florida, 1995.

Guinness Book of World Records. New York: Facts on File, 1994.

Guste, Roy F. *Antoine's Restaurant Cookbook.* New York: W. W. Norton & Company, 1980.

Hammett, Dashiell. *The Maltese Falcon.* San Francisco: North Point Press, 1984.

Hanna, Warren L. *Lost Harbor.* Berkeley: University of California Press, 1979.

Hansen, Gladys, and Emmet Condon. *Denial of Disaster: The Untold Story and Photographs of the San Francisco Earthquake and Fire of 1906.* San Francisco: Cameron and Company, 1989.

Harte, Bret. *Tales of the Argonauts and Other Sketches.* Boston: J. R. Osgood, 1875.

Hawkes, Ellen. *Blood & Wine: The Unauthorized Story of the Gallo Wine Empire.* New York: Simon and Schuster, 1993.

Holliday, James S. *The World Rushed In: The California Gold Rush Experience.* New York: Simon and Schuster, 1981.

————. *Rush for Riches: Gold Fever and the Making of California.* Berkeley: University of California Press, 1999.

Hunt Jackson, Helen. *Ramona.* New York: Grosset & Dunlap, 1884, 1912.

Ide, Simeon. *The Conquest of California by the Bear Flag Party: A Biographical Sketch of the Life of William B. Ide.* 1880; reprint, Glorieta, NM: Rio Grande Press, 1967.

Johnson, Hugh. *Modern Encyclopedia of Wine.* New York: Simon and Schuster, 1987.

Kerouac, Jack. *On the Road.* New York: New American Library, 1985.

Knox, Thomas W. *Underground, or Life Below the Surface.* Hartford: The J. B. Burr Publishing Co., 1875.

Lewis, Oscar, and Carrol D. Hall. *Bonanza Inn.* New York: Alfred A. Knopf, 1939.

Lewis, Oscar. *Bay Window Bohemia.* Garden City, NY: Doubleday & Company, 1956.

————. *San Francisco: Mission to Metropolis.* Berkeley: Howell-North Books, 1966.

Lloyd, B. E. *Lights and Shades in San Francisco.* San Francisco: A. L. Bancroft & Company, 1876.

Loewenstein, Louis K. *Streets of San Francisco.* San Francisco: Lexikos, 1984.

Marryat, Frank. *Mountains and Molehills, or Recollections of a Burnt Journal.* London: Longman, Brown, Green and Longmans, 1855.

McGloin, John. *San Francisco: The Story of a City.* San Rafael: Presidio Press, 1978.

Meler, Vjekoslav, ed. *The Slavonic Pioneers of California.* San Francisco: The Slavonic Pioneers of California, 1932.

Montagne, Prosper. *Larousse Gastronomique: The Encyclopedia of Food, Wine and Cookery.* New York: Crown Publishers, Inc., 1961.

Morgan, A. W. San Francisco Directory, 1852.

Muscatine, Doris. *A Cook's Tour of San Francisco.* New York: Charles Scribner's Sons, 1963.

————. *Old San Francisco, from Early Days to the Earthquake.* New York: G.P. Putnam's Sons, 1975.

Muscatine, Doris, Maynard Al Amerine and Bob Thompson, eds. *The Book of California Wine.* Berkeley: University of California Press/Sotheby Publications, 1984.

Neuhas, Eugene. *The Art of the Exposition.* San Francisco: Paul Elder and Company, 1915.

Oliver, Raymond. *The French at Table*. Translated by Claude Durrell. London: The Wine and Food Society, 1967.

Parry, Albert. *Garrets and Pretenders*, rev. ed. New York: Dover Publications, 1960.

Picot, Leonce, ed. *Restaurants of San Francisco*. Ft. Lauderdale: Gourmet International, 1963.

Pinney, Thomas. *A History of Wine in America, from the Beginnings to Prohibition*. Berkeley: University of California Press, 1989.

Schopp, Claude. *Alexandre Dumas: Genius of Life*. Translated by A. J. Koch. New York: Franklin Watts, 1988.

Soulé, Frank, John H. Gihon, and James Nisbet. *The Annals of San Francisco*. San Francisco: D. Appleton & Company, 1855.

Stellman, Louis. *Sam Brannan: Builder of San Francisco*. New York: Exposition Press, 1954; reprint, Fairfield, CA: James Stevenson Publisher, 1996.

Stevenson, R. L. *San Francisco: A Modern Cosmopolis*. 1882; reprint, San Francisco: Book Club of California, 1963.

Tanner, Marcus. *Croatia: A Nation Forged in War*. New Haven: Yale University Press, 1977.

Teiser, Ruth, and Catherine Harroun. *Winemaking in California*. New York: McGraw-Hill, 1983.

Thompson, Bob, and Hugh Johnson. *The California Wine Book*. New York: William Morrow and Company, 1976.

Tilden, Joe. *Joe Tilden's Recipes for Epicures*. San Francisco: A.M. Robertson, 1907.

Toklas, Alice. *The Alice B. Toklas Cook Book*. New York: Harper & Row, 1954.

Unterman, Patricia, and Stan Sesser. *Restaurants of San Francisco*. San Francisco: Chronicle Books, 1988.

Van der Zee, John. *The Gate: The True Story of the Design and Construction of the Golden Gate Bridge*. New York: Simon and Schuster, 1986.

Wait, Frona Eunice. *Wines and Vines of California*. San Francisco: The Bancroft Company, 1889.

Wells, Evelyn. *Champagne Days of San Francisco*. New York: D. Appleton-Century Company, 1939.

Willan, Anne. *Great Cooks and Their Recipes, from Taillevent to Escoffier*. London: Pavilion Books, 1992.

Writers' Program of the Works Progress Administration in Northern California. *San Francisco: The Bay and Its Cities*. American Guide Series. New York: Hastings House, 1940.

Zelayeta, Elena. *Elena's Favorite Foods California Style*. Englewood Cliffs, NJ: Prentice-Hall, 1967.

IMAGE PERMISSIONS

Text Permissions

For permission to reprint passages from other works, grateful acknowledgment is given:

To William Coblentz, Trustee of the Herb Caen Estate, for permission to reprint material appearing on pages 55, 56, 57, 58, 90, and 91 from *Baghdad by the Bay* (Garden City, NY: Doubleday & Company, 1949) and *The Best of Herb Caen* (San Francisco: Chronicle Books, 1991).

To Chronicle Books and Patricia Unterman, for permission to reprint material appearing on page 97 from *Restaurants of San Francisco* by Patricia Unterman (San Francisco: Chronicle Books, 1988).

To Harold Matson Co., Inc., for permission to reprint material appearing on pages 48 and 49 from *Champagne Days of San Francisco* by Evelyn Wells, copyright © 1937 by Evelyn Wells, renewed 1967 by Evelyn Wells.

To HarperCollins Publishers Inc., for permission to reprint material appearing on page 59 from *The Alice B. Toklas Cook Book* by Alice B. Toklas (New York: Harper & Row, 1954).

To Doris Muscatine, for permission to reprint material appearing on pages 42, 70, and 71 from her *A Cook's Tour of San Francisco* (New York: Charles Scribner's Sons, 1963).

To Penguin Putnam Inc., for permission to reprint material appearing on page 89 from *On the Road* by Jack Kerouac, copyright © 1955, 1957 by Jack Kerouac, renewed © by Stella Kerouac, renewed © 1985 by Stella Kerouac and Jan Kerouac. Used by permission of Viking Penguin, a division of Penguin Putnam Inc.

To Random House, Inc., for permission to reprint material appearing on page 58 from *To Begin Again* by M. F. K. Fisher (New York: Pantheon Books, 1992).

To the *San Francisco Chronicle*, for permission to reprint material appearing on pages 90, 91, and 106 from columns by Herb Caen dated February 17, 1970; March 24, 1995; and December 12, 1996. Copyright © by the *San Francisco Chronicle*. Reprinted with permission.

INDEX